SAYING GOOD-BYE

You &
Your Aging Parents

SAYING GOOD-BYE

You &
Your Aging Parents

by DAVID KLEIN, Ph.D.

San Francisco, California
BROWNTROUT PUBLISHERS

Library of Congress Cataloging-in-Publication Data

Klein, David H.
    Saying good-bye : you and your aging parents / David Klein.
        p.   cm.
    ISBN 1-56313-906-5
    1. Aging parents—United States—Psychology.   2. Aging parents—
Care—United States.   3. Aging parents—United States—Family
relationships.   4. Adult children—United States—Psychology.
5. Adult children—United States—Attitudes.   6. Communication in
the family—United States.   I. Title.
HQ1064.U5K478   1997
306.874—dc21
                                                                97-23098
                                                                    CIP

CONTENTS

INTRODUCTION

THE TWO GOOD-BYES

We say good-bye to our parents twice – not only when they die, but also when we begin to realize that they can no longer be the competent, vital caregivers they were in our childhood and youth. This book is for adult children who are in the process of saying good-bye – for adult children whose parents are becoming increasingly dependent on them for help and nurturance, as well as for adult children who are mourning their parents' approaching death.

As our parents age, they need our love and support in ever-increasing ways. This reality is difficult to accept on an emotional level for a number of reasons. First of all, we tend to hold on to the image of our parents as independent, nurturing, and protective. No matter how self-sufficient we become as adults, we still tend to think of our parents as our caretakers. It is difficult to give up the illusion that our parents will always have the strength, not only to deal with the issues that affect their lives, but also to care for and support us. It is difficult to let go of the belief that we can always depend on them, and we become frightened by the feeling that they are becoming increasingly dependent on us.

Second, accepting this reality involves stepping out of one time-worn role and assuming an unfamiliar, quite different role. We must go from the illusion of being a child who is protected from a cruel and difficult world to the reality of being an independent adult who no longer requires protection – an adult who must now become the protector of those who once protected him. For too many of us, clinging to a childish self-image is the source of potentially tragic denials and misperceptions about our parents' decline. Even when we put this childhood image aside, we are daunted by the prospect of having to help the very parents upon whom we once depended. This change of roles is a complex process at best. Not everyone gives up the childish fantasy of safety and freedom from responsibility. Some manage to do so only with great difficulty, while a lucky few may find that they have made the transition to full adulthood already.

Third, making this transition becomes even more complicated emotionally when we are forced to confront the idea of our own mortality. When the illusion of being cared for and protected by our parents fades, and we begin to develop a more objective understanding of our parents' needs and of the responsibility that has befallen us, we cannot help but realize that their death is inevitable – death, the second good-bye, and the last. As we consider our parents' approaching death, we come to see ourselves and even our children as part of a larger process. Previously, our parents cared for us; now, we slowly begin to care for them. After our parents pass on, we will assume their role and become elderly ourselves; eventually, our children will care for us. In this way, the aging and death of our parents foretells the approach of our own aging and death.

Recognizing the part we play in this larger process is painful for most of us. To avoid or deny it, however, as some do, is to miss out on aspects of our lives that are fundamental to our humanity. This book is based on the principle that we as adult children have a responsibility to help our aged parents to thrive and to maintain the highest possible quality of life as they gradually decline and die. In order to live up to this responsibility, we must get beyond our illusions and our conflicts. We must let go of old patterns of thinking and behaving and take on new ones, so that we can give our elderly parents the attention and nurturance that they require. We must not be overwhelmed by our new practical and emotional burdens. We must recognize that these changes are part of the great cycle of life. Our parents have passed on the role of caretaker to us; one day, we will pass that role on to our own children. We must care for our aged parents in respectful and meaningful ways, not only to honor our duty to them, but also to honor our duty to our own children. We must set an example for our children to follow, so that they, too, can become fully adult when it is their turn to care for us.

This book is a guide for all adult children who must confront the difficulties of trying to help their elderly parents. It is based on my own painful struggle to come to terms with my parents' aging and death, as well as on some inspiring and sometimes heartbreaking stories of people I have encountered both professionally and personally. This book is about recognizing our changing roles and dealing with our reactions to them, so that we can rise to the challenge and be there for our aging parents. It is about managing the pitfalls and twists that might cause problems along the way. It is, in effect, a journey in which we learn about our parents and ourselves – a journey that is forward-looking and human in scope, and essential to the continuity of life.

Our journey begins in Chapter 1 with the study of a positive and healthy relationship between an aged parent and an adult child. Sol, age 89, and his son Barry, age 44, have learned to view each other realistically. These two are capable of working through a variety of difficult and sensitive issues. Father and son do not always agree, of course, but they *communicate openly*. As a result, they are able to meet the challenges of the aging process with sensitivity and trust.

In contrast to this positive relationship, we have in Chapter 2 the case of Vivien and her daughter Susan. As Vivien gradually aged and died, Susan wanted to care for her, but she was encumbered by hurt and anger from the past. These *unresolved feelings* had long influenced Susan's attitude towards her mother, and to the end their relationship remained strained and difficult. Miscommunication and estrangement compromised the quality of Vivien's life while she was dying, and left her daughter guilt-stricken afterwards.

As our journey continues, we confront the necessity of making an *objective assessment* of the changes in our parents' lives. We must identify the physical, emotional, and attitudinal needs of our aged parents before we can deal realistically and pragmatically with the issues surrounding their increasing debility. We must separate our own needs from those of our aged parents, and we must put our parents' needs first. In Chapters 3, 4, and 5, we examine how several adult children faced these challenges, some more successfully than others.

We must be aware of our aged parents' progressive physical dysfunction. It is so easy to *deny reality* – to miss the fact, for example, that our parents are no longer feeding themselves adequately or managing their medications competently. If we are to recognize such changes, we must engage in careful and ongoing scrutiny of our parents' condition – a duty which, for various emotional or practical reasons, many adult children neglect. Furthermore, once we recognize our parents' deficiencies, we must *take action* to accommodate them, and many of us find doing so both inconvenient and emotionally difficult. Yet our role as adult children cannot be evaded. We must become aware of the many support services available to ourselves as well as to our aged parents, and we must work to get past the psychological issues that prevent us from intervening meaningfully on our parents' behalf.

The practical decisions we make have a tremendous *emotional impact* on both our parents and ourselves. Objective observation, planning, and intervention are not the only factors that are critical in maintaining our aged parents' quality of life. Courage and sensitivity are also required, not only to deal with our own anxieties and frustrations, but also those of our aged parents.

Here, and indeed throughout our journey, we encounter the importance of *emotional attitude.* Our biological destiny is to a large extent fixed; how we deal with the physical realities of aging and debility is another matter. Our aging parents can make specific lifestyle choices that will help them function more effectively. We all know middle-aged people who behave as if they were a great deal older than their age suggests; conversely, we know elderly people who act much younger than their years – for example, octogenarians who still jog and socialize. One major factor that accounts for such lifestyle differences is attitude. If a person identifies himself as old and therefore incapable, he literally creates a condition that makes him feel older than he is. It is possible, however, to accept age-related decline and still develop a positive outlook. Attitudes can change – a psychological truth that many overlook. A healthier attitude can make all the difference in maintaining a high quality of life. If our parents learn to approach the aging process positively, they can improve their physical as well as their emotional well-being. We must do everything we can to facilitate this, such as finding activities and projects that will keep our parents lively and interested. Depression is common in the elderly because of dysfunction and isolation; but so, too, is boredom. We must guard against allowing our parents to slip into a withdrawn, isolated existence where they simply mark time. This, too, is part of our responsibility as adult children.

Next in our journey, we encounter death and dying. Losing a parent to death involves a major adjustment for the adult children left behind. We must deal with our initial shock; we must pass through a variety of feeling states that include denial, guilt, anger, sadness, depression, and eventual acceptance. While memories of our parents live on in our minds and in our hearts, we must come to accept the fact that their physical presence is gone forever. This is no small adjustment, and it is one that should be understood and dealt with as honestly as possible.

In the last chapter, as well as at the end of each chapter, we look at my own dear mother, Rose, and the journey I took as I learned to deal with her increasing debility and eventual death. These recollections were meaningful for me to write, and I hope you will find them meaningful, too. It is most important that you recognize that you are not alone as you face the difficulties of saying good-bye to your aging parents. Many of us have gone through or are going through the same process; there is much empathy and understanding about this phase of life all around you. I hope this book will help you to open up and share your experiences with family and friends, as you proceed in your journey through this rough but ultimately life-enhancing terrain.

Of course, every parent ages differently, and every individual has a personal and idiosyncratic life history. When we examine a variety of stories and experiences, however, themes emerge that apply in almost every case, as you will see. These themes bear enormously on our success or failure as the caretakers of our elderly parents.

The Theme of Communication

Communication between parents and children is never easy, and never to be taken for granted. As parents age, communication becomes even more difficult. Many elderly parents are reluctant to talk openly about their concerns and anxieties, and many resist relinquishing their old positions of authority and autonomy. We adult children must be alert to such problems when we communicate with our aged parents. We must learn how to listen to them, how to pick out from their normal conversations the clues that tell us what they really feel and what they really want us to do for them.

The Theme of Unresolved Feelings

Our aged parents are, after all, our parents; it is normal to have complex and ambivalent feelings about them. We must begin to deal with these feelings before we can act sensitively and effectively on our parents' behalf. Even if we cannot resolve our old conflicts or fully break the behavioral patterns that we carry with us from the past, we must learn to recognize them and to prevent them from obstructing our efforts to give our parents the best quality of life.

The Theme of Illusion Versus Objectivity

Again, our aged parents are still our parents; it is natural to harbor illusions about them. Many of our ideas about our parents evolve in childhood, when we see them as able and effective adults. But these ideas, carried over into adulthood, may obscure the reality of our aged parents' physical decline. As much as we may wish it to be otherwise, our aged parents are no longer the vital caregivers they were when they were younger. Clinging to illusions about them prevents us from understanding what they are going through now. We must try to be objective about our parents' condition, so that we may provide the care and support that they need.

The Theme of Emotional Sensitivity

If we find it difficult to accept our parents' decline and approaching death, imagine how difficult it must be for them! It is critical that we tend to our parents' emotional needs at this time. When our parents took care of us, they did not neglect our emotional lives; now that we are their caretakers, we must be sensitive to this side of their experience. The importance of fostering a vital, positive, and life-affirming attitude in our aged parents must not be underestimated.

The Theme of Action

Our aged parents may not have many years left. Any day may prove to be their last. Elderly people undergo sudden and drastic changes in their physical abilities, as well as slow and relatively predictable ones. In either case, it is well to plan ahead, to formulate plans for our parents' future in an open and communicative atmosphere. Whatever we can do to resolve the difficulties in our relationship with our parents, we must do *now*. Whatever actions we can take to improve the quality of their lives, we must take *now*.

The Theme of Our Own Well-Being

We are likely to experience many complex and ambivalent emotions as we say good-bye to our aged parents. At this stressful time, when our own needs must come second, it is important that we find appropriate ways to release steam and to work through our own emotional issues. It is helpful to speak honestly to confidantes with whom we can trust our deepest secrets. Keeping feelings inside will only impede our effectiveness as caretakers and make our own lives more difficult. Our emotional well-being has a powerful influence on the actions we take or fail to take on behalf of our aged parents. Moreover, the memory of our success or failure as adult children will stay with us long after our parents our gone.

These, then, are our themes and our approach. Let us begin our journey.

My mother was a kind and nurturing person. When misfortune struck a neighbor or a friend, she was always the first to say, "How can we help?"

I remember one incident from my childhood that affected my entire life. I was in third grade, and we were studying Native Americans. I did not know much about the topic, but the other kids in my class seemed to know a lot. They raised their hands and volunteered information while I just sat there and listened. I began to feel awkward and stupid. They knew so much, and I knew so little! I was too ashamed to seek help from my teacher or my friends. I was afraid that if I confessed my ignorance, they would laugh at and reject me. As a result, I kept my feelings to myself. Gradually, they began to intensify. I lay awake at night and worried about class the next day.

Soon, I developed stomachaches and headaches. Some were deliberately faked, so I could avoid going to school. Others felt like real symptoms, but they served the same purpose. Initially, my mother believed that I was sick and allowed me to stay home from school or to come home early. After a while, she began to suspect that my behavior stemmed from an emotional conflict. One day, she sat me down and gently asked what was troubling me. Right away, I denied that anything was wrong. As she persisted in trying to draw me out, however, I began to cry, then sob, then wail. She had tapped into feelings of frustration, insecurity, and anxiety that I had suppressed for weeks. At first, my mother simply encouraged me to release my emotions. Then, she reassured me that I was not stupid and that there was no cause for embarrassment. Finally, she helped me find a way out of my dilemma. The very next day, we went to the library together after school, and soon I was raising my hand in class, too.

I often think back to that incident because it revealed so much about my mother. It demonstrated her ability to identify feelings and to assist in bringing them out. She did not sense something and simply overlook it, as so many of us do. When she suspected that I was troubled, she pursued this intuition with delicacy and strength of purpose, even though she had no idea about the substance of my worries. Her ability to feel deeply and to communicate effectively was so strong! I believe it was her example that led me to pursue a helping profession.

Let us now now skip forward three decades.

My mother was suffering from the early stages of Alzheimer's disease. She was not overtly symptomatic; her functioning was slipping just enough to frighten her, but not enough for those around her to notice. Shopping for food had always been a regular part of her daily life, but now she began to forget the names of the people in the shops she had frequented for over 50 years. Sometimes, she would forget what she had come to purchase; other times, she would leave her purchases behind. These episodes of forgetting occurred once or twice a week — not often enough to show a pattern.

My mother was understandably distraught. She took measures to avoid further episodes. She would not shop every day, but only on the days when she was sure that she was lucid. She also began to ask neighbors to pick things up for her. Eventually, she became reluctant to go shopping at all.

My mother did not reveal her troubles to my father or to her friends because she did not want to worry them. She had seen her own mother slip into senility; she was both frightened for herself and aware of the burden on others that her own decline could become. She kept her feelings inside. As a result, they began to intensify, and she became overreactive.

Around that time, I came home to visit my parents for ten days. One day, my mother and I went shopping together. As we began to walk the familiar route home, she suddenly stopped and said, "Davey, I don't know how to get home." At first, I thought she was joking, but she continued to voice her distress, and I realized that she was serious. Gently, I tried to reassure her that we were going the right way. I reminded her that many of us forget important things. In short, I rationalized the episode and passed it off. Afterwards, however, I had a nagging feeling that this was not simply an isolated occcurrence, but perhaps a sign of something more insidious.

A few days later, I confronted my mother gently, trying hard not to display my own anxiety. She reacted defensively, offering rationalizations. "I was just a little tired," she said. "At my age, being a bit forgetful is normal. You are making too big a deal out of this." As I continued to question her, however, she began to tell me about the episodes and about how much they had frightened her. Eventually, she unburdened herself of her worries, and together we began to face the reality of her condition.

During this conversation, I encountered on an emotional level what I had only previously had the courage to face intellectually: that my mother was no longer the strong, insightful nurturer she had been all of my life; rather, she was an elderly person trying to cope with her weaknesses and her fears, and now she needed me to care for her, as she had once cared for me. It was my turn to be the caregiver – our roles had reversed.

Later that day, in a private moment, I made the following vow: I must show my mother the same sensitivity that she showed me as a child; I must try to sense and understand what she is going through; I must encourage her to release her feelings; and I must find a way to help her cope with her decline. I must imitate her example as a parent, and do my best to nurture her and to maintain the quality of her life.

I had begun to say the first good-bye.

CHAPTER ONE

THE IMPORTANCE
OF CONNECTING

This chapter will look at the relationship between Barry, a 44-year-old writer, and Sol, his 89-year-old father. Their story represents almost a prototype of an open, loving, and practical relationship between an adult child and an aged parent.

Through hard work and good fortune and, perhaps, the accident of compatibility and like temperament, Barry and Sol have succeeded in establishing an easy intimacy that has sustained their relationship across a variety of life events. This does not mean that they always agree or get along. Far from it. They often disagree and sometimes even resent each other for being difficult and overbearing. However, when there is a conflict, they are able to recover from it. That is to say, the quarrel does not sway them from the more important issue of being connected, and they are able to center their relationship no matter what obstacle arises. At times, they must agree to disagree; at other times, they can compromise. Whatever happens, they stay connected and share an unspoken, perhaps undefined, goal: to maintain their relationship.

Most of us are not as fortunate as these two people. Not all of us possess the flexibility that is the hallmark of Barry's and Sol's relationship. To varying degrees, our own imperfections and those of our aged parents protrude into the relationship. There are a myriad of variations among us in this regard. Sometimes, the child is flexible and the parent rigid; sometimes, a flexible parent encounters a rigid child. Sometimes, of course, both are rigid. Wherever we find ourselves or our aged parents, we must not remain stuck or mired. Rather, we must always work for positive change, even when this involves sacrifices on our part.

First, of course, we must assess our relationship with our aged parents. We must identify its strengths and weaknesses. We must work to change those aspects that are hurtful or dysfunctional and to nurture those that are promising and positive. We must take stock of the relationship, come to understand what is right and what is not, and act to change what needs changing. The story of Barry and Sol provides an example of what we all may be able to accomplish if we are willing to do what it takes to maintain a positive, open, dynamic relationship with our aged parents.

Sol was born in 1907. His parents were Hungarian immigrants who fled persecution and poor economic conditions. Sol's parents had the insight to perceive how limited the opportunities were in their native land as well as the vision and courage to sail away and establish a new life in America.

Once settled in America, Sol's father sold textiles from a pushcart while his mother cooked for people and took in sewing. Sol and his five siblings were born in this country. They grew up in a poor home, but Sol remembers that his basic needs were always met. By today's standards, it was a hard existence. All six children slept in the same bed. Everyone worked as soon as they were able. Education was highly valued, but contributing to the family's livelihood was necessary for survival. As a young boy, Sol shined shoes and cleaned stores. He rarely had time to play. Sol does not remember this as a bad time, however. He feels that his family was closely knit and loving. In fact, he remembers those days as being a lot of fun, although, as he looks back now, he is astounded that he lived the way he did.

As a young adult, Sol got a job as a salesperson in a company that sold textiles to manufacturers of clothing. His enthusiasm, positive attitude, and willingness to work hard made him stand out among even the most experienced sales staff. Sol shared his success with his family. In fact, throughout his life, he has never turned away a family member or friend in need. At times, his generosity was exploited, as when a brother-in-law borrowed a significant sum of money and then failed to pay it back, denying that he had ever borrowed it. Most of the people he helped were honest and fair, however, and helping those in need increased Sol's sense of self-worth.

During World War II, Sol was too old for active duty, so he served as a civilian ambulance driver. In the late 1930s, he married and had his first child. Some years later, he had his second. It is his third child, Barry, born in 1952, who concerns us here, for Sol's and Barry's relationship has developed and maintained those special qualities in which we are interested.

Barry was the youngest child, often referred to by Sol as the "baby." Barry clearly is Sol's favorite child. When I asked Sol why this is so, he gave a rather interesting answer. Sol had been a middle child. However, his youngest sibling, Phil, was very special to him. Sol had looked after his baby brother and loved him dearly. Phil, as a young boy, worked in a laundry transporting wet towels up several flights of stairs to the roof, where they dried in the air. It was a physically taxing job, yet Sol reports that his little brother worked without complaint.

One day, Phil became ill and was taken to a hospital. Sol remembers being told that his brother had a heart condition that had worsened suddenly, but had been present all of his life. Not long after his hospital stay, Phil died. Sol was devastated and, to this day, some 65 years later, still finds his eyes filling up with tears whenever he relates the story. He still feels pain and sadness about the loss of his baby brother. He blames himself to some extent, because he allowed Phil to carry those heavy loads up the stairs, even though at the time he thought the job was too hard for so young a boy.

It is hardly surprising, then, that Sol should have a special relationship with the "baby" in his own family. When sharing the dimension of closeness with Barry that he shares with no one else, Sol reencounters the special closeness he felt with Phil. In this way, he is able to assuage his feelings of loss and remorse. His need to reconnect and make amends to his youngest brother strengthens his bond with his youngest son. Thus, Sol has a special connection to Barry that emanates from an earlier, important relationship in Sol's life.

Sol spent a lot of time with Barry when he was a small child. He would walk him in his stroller, read him stories, and take him to museums and the zoo whenever he could. Often, his other children would go along on these excursions, but the "baby" demanded more attention and was always the focal point for Sol. As Barry grew older and became more peercentered, he and his father had less reason to spend time together. Nevertheless, Sol continued to refer to Barry as "Baby" or "Baby Boy" and, in fact, still does.

Barry has surprisingly few specific memories of his childhood. His general impression is one of growing up in a loving, nurturing home in which he was often the center of attention. He cannot specifically recall the trips to the zoo and museums, but rather has jumbled them into a sort of memory lump in which he did a lot of things with his father that were mostly positive.

Barry has one main gripe with Sol's behavior, however. This involves the fact that Sol has always seen Barry as a superachiever, as someone who is the best at whatever he does. While this is truly Sol's perspective, it is, of course, distorted. Though Barry has always done many things well, it would be impossible for him to measure up to his father's idealization. During Barry's early years, Sol's image of his favorite son was a form of pressure that gave Barry a sense of being somehow inadequate. As he grew to adulthood, however, Barry came to understand his father's distortions, and they are now merely an annoyance that crops up from time to time. In fact, this is the most common conflict between them: Sol idealizes whatever Barry does and Barry must keep his balance and distinguish their differing perspectives.

For example, Barry recently had a book of stories published by a university press. This is certainly an achievement to be proud of and to feel good about. Sol, however, views the book as a work of genius guaranteed to win his son immortal fame. He boasts about Barry as if he had achieved the standing of William Faulkner or Ernest Hemingway. While it is possible that Barry's book will advance his career, it is unlikely that a small volume of stories with a limited distribution could lead to the kind of success that Sol already treats as real. Barry admits that he fantasizes about such things from time to time, but he has a strong sense of reality regarding what such a volume's being published really means. At one time, he would have measured himself by his father's fantasies and felt himself falling short, but now he bears with his father but does not give him the credence he once did.

Sol's and Barry's differing perspectives on this issue illustrate their differing world views. Sol grew up in a family that revered learning, but whose main thrust was survival; from this perspective, having a book published is a momentous event. Moreover, Sol has no reality base upon which to gauge his son's achievement. His knows about publishing only through the media, so his contact with this realm is limited to successful authors and books. In addition, when Sol was young and struggling to rise from poverty, he sometimes dreamed of being a quiet scholar and writer. Thus, when his favorite son publishes a book, Sol is naturally apt to go overboard about it.

Barry, on the other hand, has known many writers who have pub-lished books and is aware of how competitive the field is. He knows that every year thousands of published books fail both financially and critically. Nevertheless, in his heart he hopes, of course, that his work will be acclaimed and successful. Hence, he must take care to distinguish his father's unrealistic perspective, which is valid simply because it is his point of view, from his own fantasies, and at the same time stay rooted in his own reality base. This is not an easy thing to accomplish, and Barry's book might have become a destabilizing influence in his relationship with his father. But Barry has refused to let this happen – he does not let his occa-sional annoyance at his father's fantasies get in the way of the special close-ness between them.

Similar issues occur for most of us to some degree in our relation-ships with our aged parents. Our parents have views about who we are and what we have done that differ from ours. Indeed, part of being a parent is finding a way of adjusting fantasies about the children to the reality-based data that emerges from their lives. Some parents do this better and more effectively than others, but in all cases our parents' continued expectations and disappointments affect the relationships we have with them as they age. It takes work, insight, and flexibility to come to terms with these dif-ficulties, especially when our parents' viewpoints diverge drastically from reality or from our own. Because Barry has come to understand Sol, this potential obstacle in their relationship has reached a point of responsible accommodation, allowing both valid but conflicting viewpoints to coex-ist. The key to Barry's success is his ability to put his relationship with his father first, ahead of his own feelings of annoyance and frustration.

Ironically, while we must adapt to our parents' expectations of us, it is also crucial that we adjust our expectations of our aged parents. We must surrender our illusions about them, as well as openly communicate with them about their decline and growing limitations. For example, Sol, who was once a formidable athlete, can no longer function as he used to. That is not to say that he is infirm, for he is not. He can care for himself, and he can walk fairly long distances, such as on the golf course, where he still refuses to use a cart. However, his stamina and pace are reduced. Whereas Barry can remember times when Sol played 18 holes of golf and then spent the rest of the day playing baseball with his children, Sol now needs to rest after his golf game. In fact, a round of golf leaves him so fatigued that the rest of his day is devoted to quiet activities, such as reading the paper and taking naps. Thus, Barry has had to adjust his childhood image of his father to the fact that his father is 89 years old. Though Sol is in remarkable physical condition for someone of his advanced age, he still must be looked upon as a vigorous older person and not the father Barry remembers from childhood.

All of us need to come to grips with this reality, but it is not easy to do so. It seems that many adult children recognize the changes in their aged parents only when some dramatic event occurs, such as a heart attack or a significant memory lapse. We must strive to recognize changes before they become so dramatic, for in this way we may be able to prevent some potential disaster from occurring.

I am reminded of an interview I saw on a local television news program. An older parent had been injured in a house fire and was in critical condition. A news reporter was interviewing the son, who appeared somewhat dazed as he explained what had caused the disaster. Apparently, his aged father had left a fire burning in the fireplace that evening. He had forgotten to put the fire out before going to bed and had not closed the fireplace screen or glass doors. When the father was awakened by the smoke alarm, he was somewhat confused. Eventually, he attempted to put out the fire himself rather than leave the building. As a result, he sustained significant injuries and could have died. The son just tearfully kept repeating, "I thought he could handle it on his own." If the son had had a more realistic view of his father's level of functioning, perhaps this tragedy could have been prevented. Here is a lesson for all of us: *a failure to differentiate between old memories and present realities can have dire consequences.*

We must get beyond our illusions about our aged parents so that the relationship itself can be based on accurate perceptions. Only when we have surrendered our old image of our parents can we have realistic conversations about who they are and how they live; only then can we be fully in touch. When we hold on to our illusions about our parents, we apply subtle pressure for them to comply with our expectations. Thus, honest communication falls by the wayside.

I recall a friend whose widowed father appeared to be losing weight. When confronted, he assured her that this was not the case and that he was eating a healthy diet. It was only when he developed the symptoms of anemia and was forced to see a doctor that she learned the truth. Her father had restricted his diet to small amounts of vegetables and rice. He was not eating enough to maintain his body weight and was missing certain important nutrients, such as iron. When she asked him why he had changed his diet, he replied that the price of food had gone up; if he spent too much money on food, he would have little left to leave to her as an inheritance! Having learned the truth about her father's thinking processes, my friend could then accommodate to his distortions and did so by stocking her father's refrigerator regularly. She understands now that her image of him as a strong, independent individual had blinded her to his present condition. Now, she evaluates his status periodically, by communicating more directly and openly and asking appropriate questions.

All of us must watch for this tendency to fool ourselves about our aged parents. We must communicate openly and directly if we are to relate to them in a responsible and meaningful way. Only then will we have a realistic understanding of who they are and how they live. Because Barry has been able to surmount certain difficulties in communicating with Sol, he is able to make a realistic assessment of his aging father's physical condition. By exploring how these two deal with conflicts when they arise, we can learn more about the benefits of open communication.

Sol and Barry often disagree on a variety of issues. How could they not, given their widely divergent life experiences? Their disagreements, however, never create a rift. They never allow misunderstandings or differences of opinion to weaken or divert their connection to each other.

This is an achievement well worth striving for. Many family members find it difficult to agree to disagree or would rather let old wounds fester than work to heal them. Many of us know of a parent and child who have refused to talk to each other for years. Sometimes, it is even difficult to conjure up the original reason for the rift, but the two nonetheless remain mired in negative feelings which have become a pattern of relating, or, shall we say, of *not* relating. As with many factors in adult child-aged parent relations, such a pattern can have dire consequences.

One situation I encountered, involving a misunderstanding between father and son, may serve to illustrate this point. The father owned and ran a garage. The son had worked there since high school and had eventually reached the level of Assistant Manager. It was the father's intention to have his son take over the business. However, as the son became more assertive in the operation of the business, his aging father began to resent him. The son, who had always listened to and respected his father, now often loudly denounced his business practices as old-fashioned. The father interpreted this as a sign of disrespect and often became angry and hurt by his son's statements. The son, in turn, felt like his father always put down his ideas and did not respect his contribution to the company. This situation progressed over a period of years, and gradually communications between the two lapsed.

Finally, the situation exploded into a major fight. The father, a World War II veteran, had traditionally closed the business on July 4th as a sign of respect. The son had mildly challenged this over the years. This time, he decided he would keep the garage open. He believed that doing so would show goodwill to the customers and bring in a lot of extra holiday business. He did not make his intent known to his father, however; he simply went to work. It was midday before his father drove by and realized what was going on. He pulled into the garage and began to shout at his son that he was showing disrespect, not only to his father, but to all Americans who had served their country. The son yelled back that the father was old-fashioned and a poor businessman. The shouting match intensified. Just when it appeared that blows would be struck, the son quit his job and left.

Some months later, the son opened a station of his own on a nearby corner and became his father's competitor. Neither spoke to the other for several years, each maintaining that the other had to apologize. Eventually, the death of a family member brought them together, and they resolved their differences. The son respected his father, and the father felt proud of his son's accomplishment in owning his own business. However, years had passed with little contact, years that could never be regained – years of intimacy irrevocably lost, as became clear when the father died shortly after the reconciliation.

The lesson here: if there are differences between you and your parent, it is necessary to see the big picture. *Keeping the relationship intact is more important than winning a fight.*

It is sometimes necessary to look for deeper mechanisms in order to repair emotional rifts. If you harbor negative feelings, what are they about? How important are they, in fact, in the context of your life? If you discover that these negative feelings remain despite your efforts to get beyond them, perhaps consultation with a professional can help determine the source of your need to hold on to them. Flexibility is central here – the ability to roll with the punches and come out on the other side, rather than allowing hurt feelings to fester and impede or consume the relationship.

Sol and Barry are able to do this. What is their secret? Simply this: they never allow themselves to lose sight of the overall picture. They recognize that no single incident or series of incidents is more important than their relationship to one another. Realizing this has allowed them to overcome differences that might otherwise have led to misunderstandings and emotional distance.

Take, for example, the fact that Barry is a vegetarian. He believes that all creatures have a right to life, and he lives in accordance with his beliefs. He eats no meat and uses no products with animal content. Sol, who was raised in a traditional, meat-eating culture, finds it difficult to understand his son's point of view. While Sol respects the animals sacrificed for his food and believes strongly that all creatures should be treated humanely, he nevertheless finds Barry's beliefs to be somewhat eccentric and hard to comprehend. Nonetheless, despite this difference in perspective, father and son have been able to find a common ground. Both believe strongly in the humane treatment of animals. Rather than using their differences as an occasion to quarrel, these two instead come together as much as they can by emphasizing the beliefs they share.

Whenever Sol and Barry have conflicting views on an issue, they seem instinctively to look for common ground. Usually, they discover that they share certain beliefs. When they focus on what they have in common, their differences seem less extreme. When they hit areas that are potentially volatile, they become even more flexible: they simply agree to disagree.

Another important element is that neither has an agenda to win the other over to his position. Instead of a win–or–lose debate, there is an open dialogue in which each person is free to express his opinion and knows that it will be treated with respect. This is a critical ingredient for any successful relationship: the ability to listen to the other person's point of view with minimal defensiveness, realizing that it is not necessary to agree.

Take, for example, their differing views on eating meat, and look at how this issue plays out operationally. Barry staunchly is against eating living creatures. Sol eats meat. First, both men express their ideas, carefully listening to each other. Then, they search for what they have in common, in this instance their shared belief in the humane treatment of animals. Now, they can discuss their disagreement as simply one aspect of a subject upon which they generally or partially agree. This modifies the interactive pattern in such a way that each can listen to the other's point of view nondefensively. Father and son agree on an important issue, so they do not have to feel alienated from one another on account of their disagreement. Sol thinks that Barry has some odd ideas, but a good heart. Barry understands that while Sol has a traditional view of eating meat, he still has sensitivity toward animals. Hence, both can relate around this topic and, though they disagree, still feel connected.

This process of mutual listening and tolerance is a model for all relationships between adult children and elderly parents. We must not focus on differences, but rather look for what is shared. When we find common ground, conflicts seem less important and less pressing. Sometimes, this can be difficult, for differences in age can lead to striking differences in perspective. The trick is not to overreact to a statement, but rather to try to understand it more fully, to ask questions and to find points of agreement. Don't stop listening! When we shut off communication with our aging parents, not only do we lose the benefit of their wisdom and experience; we also lose touch with their needs – not only do we miss the opportunity to be close with them; we miss information that might be essential for their health and well-being.

It is this ability to communicate and listen to one another whether or not they agree that allows Sol and Barry to discuss virtually any topic without fear. In fact, they have even discussed Sol's decline and eventual death. This is always a sensitive subject, even for a realist like Sol. Because of the openness of his relationship with Barry, however, Sol feels comfortable bringing it up. Sol often jokes about how long he will live, but he also accepts the fact that he could die at any time. He is in excellent health for a man his age, but he realizes that, at some point, he may not be able to care for himself without assistance. After discussing this eventuality, father and son together researched elder care facilities, weighing such variables as location, price, levels of care, and proximity to family and golf courses. Sol rejected a place that would be difficult for his sons and relatives to visit, as he did not want to be cut off from his family. He also rejected a place that was close to family members, but not near a golf course, since he recognizes that golf is an important part of his life and he wants to play for as long as he is able. The place he decided on is a short walk from the golf course he has played for years. The facility itself offers Sol as much freedom as he can handle and is capable of providing whatever level of care he needs on a temporary or permanent basis. For example, maid service is available if he needs it; he has his own kitchen, but he can eat communally if he does not want to cook or is unable. If he finds walking to shops or entertainment facilities difficult, transportation can be arranged. On the medical side, doctors are in attendance and all hospital services are next door should they be required. Meanwhile, Sol remains near his golfing buddies and close enough to his sons and relatives that they can pay him frequent visits. In addition, the burden of caring for Sol during an illness has been lifted from family members and placed on professional staff at the facility.

Here is another lesson to be learned from Sol and Barry. With the advent of federal moneys for the aged in the 1960s and 1970s, subsidies are now available for elder care facilities that offer a range of services extending from complete care to independent living with various degrees of supervision. Many large, mid-size, and even small towns now have such facilities. No longer does an adult child have to worry about his elderly parent's ability to live independently with the only alternatives being either to bring the parent into the child's home, fostering dependence, or to ship the parent off to a nursing home. Today, many options are available.

Parent and child must form a partnership, as Sol and Barry did, and investigate their options long before the need arises. This should be done with mutual respect and input – not in a crisis when things are pressured, but in a calm, rational, and above all nondefensive manner. Again, open communication is key.

There is much to be gained by acknowledging realities and planning for them. Some adult children recognize this, but mistakenly investigate care possibilities on their own without including their aged parents in the process. While every situation is unique and requires its own balance, an adult child's acting alone is often destructive. Making plans behind his parents' backs could make the adult child feel guilty and, when the time comes to discuss the results of his investigation, make the parents feel that the child is attempting to "get rid" of them. Keep in mind that many elderly parents have only the experience of their own parents and grandparents to relate to and draw upon. They remember a time when nursing homes and hospitals seemed places where the elderly were put to die. Thus, many elderly parents approach their future with fear and defensiveness. Looking into options behind their backs, even if the motivation is noble and caring, can only exacerbate such feelings and sometimes leads to open hostility and resistance.

I remember an elderly fellow I worked with who went through such a negative experience. He had functioned independently until a stroke left his mind lucid but his physical level of functioning impaired. While in the hospital recovering, he was shocked to hear his son announce that he did not believe his father could return home. The son argued that his father should go to an extended care facility and that his house should be sold and his possessions distributed among family members. Months before, the son had looked into elder care possibilities and had lovingly and thoughtfully made arrangements in case of a medical calamity, but he had done so *without consulting his father.* Thus, whereas the son was quite knowledgeable about various facilities and had adjusted to the idea of his father's entering one, the father found himself suddenly, at a very low point in life, presented with arrangements from which he had been excluded and that he naturally interpreted as hostile. The son's proposals made the father feel not only that his life was over, but also that the very people he might look to for help and comfort were in fact behind his suffering. He felt cut off, abandoned, rejected, and uncared for.

The son, of course, could not understand why his father became so agitated, especially since the facility suited his father's needs and tastes. He tried to reason with his father, but his father no longer trusted him. Fortunately, the son asked me to help. Because the father trusted me, I was able to moderate his response. I had him describe his fears and look at his son's reality-based ideas. I confirmed how well such facilities are run today and how the particular one his son had looked into might in fact afford a good quality of life. We agreed that I would go and see the place and then report my findings. The son also agreed that if I found the place inadequate, he would not advocate sending his father there. Moreover, the father would have the final say and would see the place himself before he made his decision. The facility turned out to be quite reasonable. Eventually, the father came to accept the fact that he did need care. He moved into the place and found it acceptable, and now he resides there quite happily.

My intervention defused the situation and rehabilitated the relationship between father and son. However, this traumatic miscommunication could have been avoided if the issue had been dealt with differently. If the son had begun his investigation a good deal earlier and involved his father in the process, the father would have had the opportunity to adjust to the idea along with his son; he would have been able to set aside his fears and misconceptions and come to a more realistic assessment of the care possibilities open to him. Above all, the two could have avoided a traumatic interaction that might have worsened the father's medical condition and destroyed their relationship.

All of us can learn from this story. Consider who your elderly parents are and how they may react to such ideas and realities. Make wise and planned decisions *with* them before events force such decisions upon you both. Some of us may be fortunate enough to have parents who can face such issues head on, as Sol did. More commonly, such issues will be fraught with anxieties. If you do not act openly, you may find yourself incorporated into your parents' fears, as happened to the son just described. Some of these anxieties may remain unexpressed. Adult children must strive to bring out their parents' misgivings, rather than accepting their reticence. Again, communication and dialogue are key.

Another problem in communication frequently arises with aged parents who lived through the Depression. Many such elderly people remember how their grandparents were an extra burden on the family. If your parents lived through this period, they may be afraid of becoming a burden on you. Indeed, not a few such elderly *choose death* in what they conceptualize as the interest of the family. Usually, their choice of death is disguised and emerges only in subtle ways, such as not telling family members they are ill or eating lesser amounts of food and slowly starving themselves. Although such behavior is rare, it is common enough that we adult children must be on guard for it with our own aged parents. Again, communication and objective assessment are necessary.

I am reminded of an elderly person who, upon being confined to a nursing home, gradually starved herself to death in order not to burden her family with additional expenses for her care. She was able to fool staff into thinking she was eating all of her food when she was in fact getting rid of it. By dressing carefully, she was able to conceal her weight loss. When weighed, she would hide a book or two in her clothing. In time, she lost enough weight that her health was affected, and her self-starvation was a major factor contributing to her death. Her sacrifice was based on a noble intention, however misplaced, and she was able to engineer her demise in a subtle and effective manner.

We must be on guard for such convoluted thinking. Many of our parents were affected by the Depression and other historical events, and they may be inordinately self-sacrificing. It is important for us to maintain enough contact and open communication to pick up on such themes and to prevent what is, after all, a sad conclusion to life.

Sol would not go so far as to end his life in order to ease the burden on his family, but he too was marked by his early experiences of economic hardship. He does not spend much money on himself, and he openly declares his intention not to diminish his estate. Barry has adjusted to this form of self-sacrifice very adroitly. For example, Sol loves chocolate, yet he will not buy any because he sees it as an expensive luxury item. Barry is well aware of Sol's attitude, so he never visits his father without bringing several large chocolate bars. Sol characteristically complains that Barry is foolish for wasting money on such items, but each week Barry notices that the chocolate is gone.

Recently, Sol was feeling a bit under the weather. Barry, who keeps a close watch, noticed that his father ate a healthy diet, but was not getting enough iron. Eventually, Barry figured out that Sol systematically avoided red meat, his favorite source of iron, because he thought that it was too expensive. Now, Barry makes sure that there are at least two steaks in Sol's freezer each week; this way, he can monitor whether or not Sol is eating them. He realizes that, although Sol avoids buying expensive cuts of meat, he will eat them if they are there. So here we have Barry, the vegetarian, buying steaks for his meat-eating father!

Sol and Barry have also discussed the possible circumstances around Sol's death. Sol states clearly and openly that he is not afraid to die. He feels that he has lived a good, productive life and would have few regrets if he were to pass away today. Nevertheless, he worries about *how* he will die. Sol's worst nightmare is to die a painful, lingering death, without dignity. "If I reach a point where I can no longer enjoy my life," Sol says, "where I'm suffering and can't take care of myself or my bodily functions, then why go on? I don't want to linger if I can't have any kind of existence." Sol does not want to live just to live; he wants to live only if he can maintain the quality of life that he enjoys now.

Barry and Sol have openly discussed Sol's fears, and Barry certainly understands his father's wishes. Accordingly, they have established what is called a "living will." This document, which is legal in many but not in all states, defines in clear language the circumstances under which lifesaving medical procedures should not be employed. For example, Sol's living will states that if he is brain-dead, he should be taken off life support and allowed to die naturally. It also states that no extraordinary lifesaving measures should be taken if Sol is incapacitated by a medical condition which does not permit any quality of life and from which there is no hope of recovery. In effect, Sol has spelled out for his loved ones exactly what his wishes would be if he should become unable to make his wishes known. He has defined the point at which he would decline medical intervention, and he has empowered Barry to act on his behalf if he is no longer able.

This document was not written lightly. Hours of discussion were held before Sol's wishes were made clear and the conditions defined. Both Barry and Sol searched their souls in arriving at their current position. Sol expressed his desires and Barry voiced his concerns. Both opened their hearts and dialogued with each other until they reached an agreement by which they could both abide. Sol realizes that Barry may be called upon to make a decision regarding Sol's life that is wrenching and painful. Barry understands that respecting his father's wishes by allowing him to die is an act of love. He further recognizes that Sol's appointing him to act on his behalf at such a juncture is an act not only of love, but also of trust and respect. Clearly, these men have opened up to each other to the point where they can communicate about virtually any topic.

We adult children need to think about how we ourselves will handle circumstances like these. Can we discuss such issues with our aged parents and find some resolution? If we can, then a living will is something to consider. If we cannot, perhaps it is time to wonder what is missing in the relationship, what prevents us from dealing with such issues. Is there ever going to be a better time to do so than the present? *To wait until circumstances force us to act is to wait too long.* We must act now, when there is time to deal with the barriers in our relationships, so that freer communication can ensue. Some will find that they are ready to do what Barry and Sol have done; others may discover that they are a long way from being able to be that honest and open. Wherever you and your elderly parents find yourselves, *now* is the time to take steps towards helping the relationship progress. If it lacks much, it can get better; if it has a great deal going for it, ask yourself how it can be further enhanced.

Barry and Sol have even discussed Sol's funeral. Sol believes strongly that funerals benefit only the funeral industry. He believes that it is not necessary to honor his death if those around him have honored him during his life. Accordingly, he has made it clear that he wants the least expensive casket and headstone. Why, he asks, should the family be burdened with a needless expense when he is gone and cannot benefit from such choices? It is better to spend money on the living. Use the money for the family, he says. When the issue of perpetual care for his grave came up, Sol laughed. He believes it will not matter to him whether his grave is cared for or not. He believes that his life and death are part of a natural process. It seems ludicrous to hinder and tame natural forces on behalf of a dead man, whose body should decompose and give back to the natural world what it took from it.

Barry and the other members of Sol's family will respect his wishes because Sol has been so clear and even eloquent in stating them. Little is left to chance, because Sol has had the courage to discuss his decline and death openly, and because his family members, especially Barry, have listened to and dialogued with him and understand his point of view.

Sol and Barry serve as an example of what we are all striving to achieve in our relationships with our elderly parents. These two are not perfect, of course, but they teach us how communication and mutual adaptation can lead to a deeper understanding. There is much to be gained from being able to discuss our feelings openly and honestly. Open dialogue allows us to know our elderly parents better and, there-fore, to become expert at understanding their quirks and seeing to their needs. Thus, we are able to provide a better quality of life for them and to adjust more fully to the changing circumstances we must face as our parents age.

Communication and adaptation work in tandem to make us better caretakers of our elderly parents. We become more responsive and can act with better judgment and greater sensitivity when we must. It matters little where we begin in our quest for improved communication and adapta-bility, but it is most important that we set these goals and begin working towards their accomplishment now, while such goals are still reachable.

Of course, there are many issues and circumstances that we would rather not have to deal with as our aged parents decline. They will arise, however, whether we want to deal with them or not. We cannot control the various factors that cause our elderly parents to struggle, but ultimately the responsibility for managing some of them will fall upon ourselves. Will not our parents do better if they have the benefit of our input as they face these challenges? And will not our counsel be better thought out and more effective if we have discussed these eventualities openly with our parents over the years?

Have the courage, then, to take the steps necessary to enhance your relational interactions with your aged parents. Failure to communicate deprives you of closeness and leaves you with little knowledge about who your parents are and what they might wish. Worse, it might condemn you to making choices without clarity and to living with disastrous consequences. Remember how suddenly the relationship between the stroke victim and his son deteriorated even though the son had good intentions. Contrast this with Sol's and Barry's relationship and it soon becomes clear that communication is the only path to trust, sensitivity, and responsiveness, to preparation for those things we can anticipate, and to increased adaptability to new situations.

I urge you to consider the material in this chapter. Use it as a guideline by which you can gauge the relative success or failure of your own relationship. Let it help you set goals to improve a bad situation or to make a good situation even better. This is your duty to your elderly parents. It honors them and it honors you. It teaches the next generation – our children who will one day be the adult children when *we* become the elderly parents – to behave as we hope we have, in a respectful, ethical, sensitive, and meaningful way.

Alzheimer's disease is progressive. My mother deteriorated gradually. She went from a loving soul who managed the various issues in her life to a confused individual who could not make sense of things. As the disease progressed, she became increasingly needy. Her needs were not simply the obvious ones, such as help preparing her meals or supervision when she went out. They were also emotional needs. Like any of us in difficult and stressful conditions, she was afraid and apprehensive. This was exaggerated by the confusion that the disease produced in gradually and insidiously increasing ways.

My mother was good at discussing her feelings and needs once we established open communication. I remember taking her to a Broadway show, a fairly complex and symbolic play about the effects of the loss of a parent on a child at a later point in her life. I found the show very good. My mother, however, kept asking me what was going on. She had trouble following and interpreting the action. She had difficulty remembering what occurred from one scene to the next, so she was missing important information that explained why certain events were happening and what they meant. She would lean over and quietly ask, "Davey, why is this girl so sad?" or "What happened to the person in India?" Her questions revealed that she was getting some of the material, but missing most of it. She was especially aware of scenes in which great emotion was expressed. She could identify with the feelings, but she did not remember the events that led to them. Gradually, the people around us became impatient with her questions and my answers, despite the fact that we spoke in whispers. We made it through the show and went to dinner. Over dinner, my mother continued to ask questions about the show. These were not intellectual questions about the content, but rather questions that made it clear that she was still trying to make sense of individual events. She was aware that the play had evoked a lot of feelings in her; she remembered some events, but she did not have a sense of the continuity of the action, and this upset her. Patiently and painstakingly, I went through the details of the plot and helped her to figure out how they correlated with her feelings. Eventually, we pieced together the whole story line. Only then did she seem more at ease and relaxed.

I was struck by a number of things. Above all, I was aware of how much her disease limited her ability to understand. She had substance and feelings without the structure that explained and made sense of them. How confusing it must have been for her to try to make sense of the play! How much more confusing and even embarrassing life must have been for her on a daily basis!

In terms of communication, this episode was significant. Clearly, my mother and I had come a long way since we had first talked about her ongoing difficulties. Even though her condition had progressed, our ability to discuss it had greatly increased at the theater, and afterwards she felt comfortable enough to reveal her confusion fully. Because I understood her deficit, I had the patience to discuss what she needed to know in order to make sense of the show. She communicated her needs, and I understood them. She trusted me with her vulnerabilities, and I responded to her in a sensitive and supportive manner, as she had to me when I was a child. She felt understood and accepted as she was; I felt helpful and confirmed as a responsible son striving both to understand and to respond to my mother's needs. Our dialogue continued long after we went to this show. I grew in knowledge about how her thought processes operated, because the barriers of defensiveness and rationalization were down and we both felt free to express ourselves and to interact meaningfully.

Interestingly, a few months later during another visit, my mother asked me to take her to another Broadway show. Had we not striven to communicate, I might *well have turned her down, not willing to undergo the embarrassment of having a confused elderly woman constantly asking me questions during the performance. Worse, I might have taken her and become as annoyed and short-tempered as the people around us had been at the first show. Instead, because I fully comprehended her condition, I chose a show which involved a lot of sight gags and constantly changing scenes, with no real plot or dialogue. My mother could react simply to the humorous mimelike shenanigans on stage. If she missed the essence of one, the next would unfold before she had an opportunity to worry about it. This was, in effect, the ideal show for someone with my mother's deficiencies. She had a great time and laughed boisterously along with the rest of the audience. She remarked later how much she had enjoyed the show and how pleased she was that she had behaved just like everyone else. Here was this sweet woman − ravaged by a disease that was insidiously robbing her of her dignity and ability to function, a disease that often left her confused and anxious − working to help me understand what she was going through! Her ability to articulate the frightening parts of her life increased my sensitivity. Thus, I was able to accommodate to her needs and to provide positive experiences designed around her deficiencies. Furthermore, our dialogue enabled me to communicate with other significant people in her life and to help them to do the same. Communication was the key to maintaining the quality of her existence, and she was a major part of this process.*

It took courage for my mother to be so open with me about her experience of the world. She not only faced her deficiencies; she also talked about them, revealing her fragility and confusion. I came to understand her, not just based upon how she acted, but also based upon her feelings about herself. She still had the ability to be self-aware, and she communicated this self-awareness. For my part, I had to find the courage to respond to her accordingly and to extend my understanding of her to others. This was not an easy thing for either of us to pull off. We worked at it with energy and strength and love. As a result, she played an instrumental part in maintaining the quality of her life.

CHAPTER TWO

THE TRAGEDY OF NOT CONNECTING

In this chapter we will look at how an estranged mother and daughter dealt with the mother's physical and cognitive deterioration. Sad as their story is, it presents many elements common to most adult child-aged parent relationships. These elements include generational differences of perspective, ambivalent feelings of love and anger, unresolved emotional issues, and the guilt of the middle-aged child who fails to act on the aged parent's behalf to cushion the impact of increasing debility.

Susan is typical of many adult children who have strongly ambivalent feelings about their parents and deal with their conflicting emotions by remaining distant and apparently uncaring. There are usually unresolved issues lurking in such ambivalence, feelings of being unloved or less loved than a sibling, for example. Nearly all of us have some unresolved feelings remaining from childhood, but most of us accept them or at least adapt in such a way as to move ahead with our lives and responsibilities. Some adult children, however, feel pain and trauma of such magnitude or intensity that, even after years of living away from their parents, they continue to be plagued by conflictual themes. Such people feel considerable torment, which has serious repercussions for their treatment of their aged parents. Adult children who continue to reexperience childhood hurt and confusion often engage in behaviors that would appear puzzling, callous, or even brutal to an observer who does not realize the context from which such behaviors stem. Some adult children seem oblivious to the needs of their parents. Others recognize a need, but fail to act upon it because they cannot let their recognition of the need outweigh their conflicted feelings. Still others see their parents' decline as an opportunity indirectly to punish the parents for failing to take care of their own needs at an earlier time, perhaps childhood or adolescence.

The aged parents, on the other hand, wonder why the child they raised and cared for cannot somehow respond to their needs. They are likely to feel rebuffed, rejected, and in the way. They can sense the child's ambivalence, yet they cannot find the energy or courage to confront it. They might wonder, for example, as they sit alone in a chilly apartment, why their son or daughter does not offer to send them to a warmer climate for the winter, where they can be active and enjoy life. The freezing temperatures outside reflect the coldness of emotional withdrawal inside when parent and child come together. All too often, such parents do not express their feelings of disappointment in the adult child's response to their situation. They may broach such issues with a confidante; in the presence of the child, however, they discuss superficialities and pretend that all is well. Nonetheless, both parent and child are painfully aware of the tension that overshadows their encounters.

The relational pattern that has evolved over the decades is one of obligatory rather than desired contact. For the adult child, seeing the parents brings up unresolved and seemingly unresolvable issues from childhood, yet a sense of guilt and responsibility forces regular, tension-filled visits. For the aged parents, even these visits are a welcome respite from loneliness and boredom. Out of fear of being totally abandoned, the parents will not risk a direct confrontation, because it might expose the painful undercurrents that exist. They will not say out loud, "Why do you not help me?" or "What has happened between us that prevents you from responding to my needs?" Such questions are not voiced, yet their thunderous presence is felt as a strain.

Just what are these ambivalences and where do they originate? While each of us has a unique personal history, some generalizations can be made. Such feelings develop during childhood. Young children are fully dependent upon their parents for food, shelter, love, approval, and virtually life itself. How these needs are met influences how they later view the world. When parents are sensitive and loving, a feeling of safety and predictability is engendered. The child begins a gradual journey toward ever-increasing independence which eventually ends when he has acquired the skills to deal with the demands of adulthood. The parents guide and help this process.

However, if a parent is deficient in any of a variety of ways, the child may be adversely affected. When reared by a dysfunctional parent, say one addicted to alcohol, who is frequently overreactive and nonfunctional and at times abusive, the child develops a view of the world as a dangerous place. Such a child usually feels that he must care for the parent rather than the other way around. Children forced to assume roles that are beyond their abilities develop a sense of inadequacy, anxiety, and often despair. Such children view the home not as a safe haven in which to grow and mature, but rather as a place where they are hurt and overwhelmed. Their confidence is minimal and they have no sense of security. Such children may develop pathological thinking and distorted conceptualizations about how parents function and families operate. When such children reach adulthood, these experiences and ideas have a negative impact on their own relationships if they fail to recognize their dysfunction and continue to play out the behaviors learned in the original family. This is one explanation of why there is such a high incidence of alcoholism in the adult children of alcoholic parents, or why children who were abused by their parents often find themselves abusing their own children.

Thus, the patterns of childhood repeat in adulthood. When in the course of time the roles of parent and child begin to reverse and the adult children are needed to care for their aged parents, such children often have only their parents' example to draw on. If that model was dysfunctional, there is a likelihood that such adult children will be incompetent caregivers to their aged parents. In addition, unresolved feelings must be factored into the situation. If the children feel anger and resentment towards the parents for not having attended to their needs or not having provided the guidance they required, these feelings too will be acted out behaviorally. Hence, such adult children may simple say, "This lousy SOB didn't take care of me. Why should I take care of him?" Or somewhat more understandably, "I don't want to give to him because he did not take good care of me."

Such feelings can lead to behavior that ranges from abandoning the aged parents to associating with them reluctantly. Most adult children are aware of the value that society places on the obligation to care for our elderly parents. But such pressure only leads someone who is ambivalent, someone who is still haunted by childhood demons, to suffer guilt when he responds coldly or minimally to his parents' needs.

Some, of course, are able to resolve their conflictual feelings and to make reasonable choices about how to behave. In this chapter, however, we are concerned with a daughter who does not find her way out of her conflict, but rather continues to experience her ambivalence about her aged mother and behaves in a way that, consciously or unconsciously, is consistent with her feeling state. By examining in some detail the history that led Susan to treat her mother Vivien as she did, we can begin to understand how we ourselves might have emotional ambivalences towards our aged parents, and how these can affect our relations with them in complex, subtle, and possibly destructive ways.

Vivien was born in Philadelphia in 1910, eight years after her parents immigrated from Italy in search of better economic opportunities. The family did not flourish in America, but they did make ends meet. Her father was a tailor while her mother cared for the children. Although Vivien's parents never quite felt at home in America, they did acculturate somewhat, learning to speak English and becoming accustomed to the norms of this country.

Two of the children were born in Europe, and Vivien and her sister were born in the United States. The children, of course, found the transition to American culture much less difficult. With their parents holding fast to many of the values and behaviors of the old country, however, they did experience some discontinuity, an experience quite common among the children of immigrant parents. Vivien frequently felt she did not fit in. Her parents' traditional, old–world perspective clashed with that of her more modern American friends.

At 17, Vivien finished high school and became employed as a secretary in an office at a factory. One of her older sisters also worked there. Vivien earned a reasonable salary, and she and her sisters were able to contribute to the family and raise its standard of living.

At 25, Vivien married a man who came from a similar background and worked in manufacturing. Despite little formal education, he managed to earn a considerable living. When Vivien became pregnant with their only child, Susan, she gave up her job to become a full-time mother. Vivien's husband was a loving and supportive father. He spent long hours with Susan on the weekends, but during the week he worked 12 to 14 hours a day, having only minimal contact with her. Susan and Vivien, however, spent much of their days together and interacted continuously. Vivien did all that she could to care for Susan. Motherhood was the central theme in her life.

Vivien realized that children who attended the public school system, as she had, did not have the same opportunities as those who could afford to attend the private academies for which Philadelphia was famous. Indeed, those private schools were affiliated with the finest colleges in the country. Vivien believed that attending such a school would give Susan an excellent chance of being admitted to an Ivy League college, and that attending such a college would practically guarantee her daughter's economic security.

Sending Susan to private school became a goal that Vivien and her husband worked toward. Because the tuition would be a significant financial burden, they saved their money by depriving themselves of many luxuries that they could otherwise afford. Sacrifice was not a difficult concept for these people to grasp. They had come out of deprivation and, even with the restrictions they placed upon themselves, were still much better off than they had been as children, and light-years ahead of the poverty their parents had experienced in their early years. Their parents had sacrificed for them; now, they would sacrifice for their own child. They cut back expenses by buying a smaller car and simpler food. Before, Vivien and Susan went to a resort for the summer; now, they opted for only an occasional weekend away. Before, Vivien dressed herself and her daughter very stylishly; now, they went to more practical stores and bought more durable clothing. Dinner out and a movie, once regular pastimes, became less frequent. Even birthday presents, once special and elaborate, were significantly reduced in splendor.

Vivien viewed these sacrifices as a noble act. Susan, on the other hand, had a very different view. She had come to see herself as more affluent than her classmates at public school and her friends in the neighborhood. After all, she had a much larger apartment; she had finer clothes; during the summer, she swam in the lakes of a quiet resort, while others had to be content with an occasional dunk in the city's public pools. Indeed, some of Susan's school friends marveled at her lifestyle.

In other words, Susan saw herself as the envy of her peers, and had developed an identity that centered around this view. Then, suddenly, everything changed. As her parents cut back on spending in order to send her to a more affluent school, her lifestyle came to resemble that of her poorer friends. Now, she too stayed in the city during the summer and wore unstylish clothes! Her exalted self-image was thus abruptly destroyed.

Here you have two very different interpretations of the same events, a development quite common in families. While Vivien and her husband believed that they were making an important sacrifice in order to secure Susan's future, Susan perceived their new frugality as extremely destructive. Susan felt as if her world had fallen apart. Being a child, she had difficulty understanding the benefit of her parents' plan. The ideal of a better education leading to future security and prosperity did not compensate for the loss of her special position and status. Her self-image was suddenly crushed, because of choices made by her parents. As a result, she harbored a great deal of distress, anger, and resentment towards them. In this way, she became emotionally damaged by her parents' sacrifices.

Susan frequently visited with her aunt and grandmother, who lived together nearby. She witnessed how her aunts and her mother took care of her grandmother. She saw, through example, how each generation had an unspoken responsibility to offer care and nurturance to those who once cared for and nurtured them. This was a value that ran deep in the family's history. While Susan took this for granted during her early years and internalized it as normative behavior, she now, in her reduced circumstances, became painfully aware of how her parents contributed financially to the grandmother's care. She believed that her change in status could be reversed if her parents only kept the money they gave away. Susan increasingly resented her parents for making such a contribution and her grandmother for needing it. This became the beginning of a conflict that, as we will see, played itself out in Susan's life when she became an adult child charged with her aging mother's care. She had internalized the family value of caring for elderly family members, yet she also resented having to abide by it because she associated the responsibility with painful experiences.

Three and one half years after her parents' decision, Susan was enrolled at a private academy. The school catered to the rich, but had traditionally opened up a few places for partial scholarship students, and Susan became one such pupil. The school was located in a lovely parklike campus in a wealthy area, in the middle of a privately owned forest. The students belonged to the culture of the rich. They shopped at the finest stores in Philadelphia. Some arrived at school in chauffeured limousines.

Some resided in townhouses on Rittenhouse Square or other wealthy neighborhoods, and some lived on estates in nearby suburbs. In short, their lifestyle was far removed from even the one Susan had formerly believed was so privileged.

On the first day of school, Susan dressed in her best, most stylish clothes. To Vivien and her husband, this was a momentous day. They had succeeded in getting their daughter into one of the finest schools in the country and thus had given her the possibility of moving well beyond what they had achieved. For Susan, however, entering the new world of her affluent school was quite a different experience. Before, she felt insecure because she had fallen from a position of envy to an average position which she had previously viewed as beneath her. Now, she faced a far more threatening situation: being derided by peers whom she viewed as superior.

In addition, her new environment produced a sense of discontinuity in Susan. She no longer fit into the culture of her lower-middle-class neighborhood, because she was being exposed to other lifestyles and values; but she did not fit into the new culture of the rich either, because she was ignorant of its norms. Ironically, Susan's predicament resembled that of her immigrant grandparents, but in one sense her predicament was even harder, for she had no guides to fall back on. Susan's parents, who did not understand the nature of her situation, were of no real help to her. They were generally supportive, but they could not comprehend the level of distress and discomfort she was experiencing.

Two examples of Susan's confusion in her new circumstances come to mind. Susan had saved money for a long time from babysitting and allowances to buy herself a jacket, an "in" blue blazer that many of her classmates wore. Susan, of course, could not afford to purchase her jacket at the fashionable store where her peers bought theirs, and instead went to a local merchant and bought a coat that was the same color and style and fabric, but much cheaper in price. She remembers being thrilled to wear it to the next school dance. On her way to the dance, she felt increasingly confident about how "in" she looked. As she entered the hall, she thought how she might be starting to fit in at school. As she walked confidently along one side of the room, a few girls approached her. One of them commented on how nice her blazer looked. Susan felt very good about the comment until the same girl asked her where she got it and then folded down the collar to see the label! It was immediately obvious that this coat did not come from the popular, fashionable store, and the girl who had looked at the label commented loudly that she had never heard of the store and that the coat was not really so nice after all.

Susan remembers being devastated by this event. She had harbored the hope of being accepted by her peers, but instead she had been treated as an unacceptable outsider. This incident served as a symbol for all her social experiences at the school and reinforced her underlying resentment at being cast adrift by her parents in such an environment.

The second such event occurred at a later point in her schooling. Susan had befriended one of the other students who, though wealthy, nevertheless was on the fringe of social acceptability. This girl invited Susan to spend the night at her mansion, located in a beautiful section of The Main Line. Susan accepted and once again felt that perhaps this invitation signaled a turning point in her new social life. She accompanied her friend home in a limousine. She tried not to seem awestruck by the opulence she encountered at her friend's house. As she and her friend sat down at the dinner table, Susan noticed that her place setting had two forks, a long one and a short one, and she was seized with despair, for she had no idea which fork to use. While Susan did manage to muddle her way through the dinner, her ignorance of table manners remained in her mind as an example of how out of place she was in the context in which her parents had placed her.

These examples may seem like minor occurrences to some readers. To Susan, however, they symbolized her deep sense of not fitting in. They became symbols of what she encountered over and over again. A growing sense of not belonging plagued her, leaving her confused and isolated. She felt inadequate and, above all, resentful; she was furious with her parents, especially her mother, for placing her in this position and leaving her to fend for herself without the resources to succeed. This deep-seated pain and anger formed the basis of her behavior toward Vivien in later years.

In important ways, however, Vivien's decision to send Susan to a private school did pay off. Despite her social confusion, Susan obtained a fine education. When she graduated from high school, she was accepted at an Ivy League college, where she flourished both academically and socially. Her standing among her peers was markedly better at college because she had come from a private high school. In addition, the student body was larger, so there were more people like Susan who had academic credentials but did not come from established, wealthy families. In high school, she had stood out; in college, she could blend in.

Law school followed, again at an Ivy League institution. With her academic success as an undergraduate behind her, Susan was even more acceptable to her law school peers. Inside, however, she still felt alienated. Externally, she now dressed and behaved exactly as her peers did; internally, however, she still held on to the insecurities and resentment of her earlier years. For example, she never invited her classmates to visit her at her parents' apartment, because she was afraid that one look at her parents would reveal that she did not fit into her new friends' lifestyle after all. Her parents, you see, still did not know which fork to use! To Susan, they were an embarrassment, and she dreaded those times when her parents would, of necessity, encounter her peers.

Susan graduated in the top 20 percent of her law school class and was hired by a prestigious firm. Over the years, she became a prominent and wealthy attorney. Her name was often in the newspapers, and her expertise was sought by many famous and powerful people. Susan had arrived at a station in life where she was accepted in the most influential circles. Outwardly, she was bright, successful, wealthy, and powerful. Inwardly, however, the insecurities and resentment that had troubled her in her youth remained.

The years had not been so kind to Vivien, to whom age had brought considerable debility. I met Vivien near the end of her life. She came to my office twice while visiting Susan, who by then had moved out of Philadelphia with her husband and children and taken a position at a law school. It was during these two visits that I learned how life had been for Vivien. It was clear that she had not been at all aware of Susan's distress at moving from the neighborhood school to the private academy. Vivien believed that she had done the right thing for her daughter's future. Given her background, Vivien could not understand the cultural shift and ensuing confusion her daughter had experienced. She was, therefore, unable even to recognize how difficult the changes had been for Susan, no less to understand the coldness and resentment that her daughter demonstrated more and more as the years went by.

Vivien and Susan grew apart emotionally despite Vivien's attempts to play a larger part in her daughter's life. While Susan was still in high school, Vivien frequently invited her to go shopping, but more often than not Susan politely refused. For a time, Vivien subscribed to a theater club that provided her with discounted tickets to local productions. Susan would accompany Vivien to the theater, but was always reluctant to go for a meal before. Vivien also attempted to help her daughter with her school work, but the work was usually too sophisticated. At times, she suggested that Susan bring friends home for dinner or an overnight visit, but Susan always declined; she visited her friends' homes, but would not invite anyone into her own. Susan offered excuses, and each time Vivien accepted the excuse. In her heart, however, Vivien was hurt. She began to feel as if her daughter were ashamed of her. This feeling was reinforced by the way Susan discouraged her parents from getting involved in school events. When her parents did go to the school to see Susan perform in a play or concert, Susan was clearly uncomfortable and usually wanted to leave as soon as the event ended.

Because she was not adept at confronting emotional issues, Vivien held her feelings inside. As time progressed, contact between Vivien and Susan became quite minimal. There were weekly phone calls to keep in touch, but fewer visits. When Susan graduated and returned to Philadelphia after her father's death, there were more visits, but they remained sporadic and always had an edge of tension. Vivien, of course, had no idea of the level of resentment and pain that Susan had carried since childhood, and attributed Susan's distance to her different lifestyle. When Susan had children, contact became somewhat more frequent until Susan moved away. Then Vivien visited only from time to time, and even this infrequent contact was somewhat cold and emotionally distant.

Vivien's health problems began at age 59, when she had a massive heart attack from which she was not expected to recover. Susan came to see her mother in the hospital. She remembers having many mixed and confusing feelings. On the one hand, she felt afraid that her mother would die and thus she would lose her mother's unconditional positive regard. On the other hand, she felt a growing sense of relief because soon her mother would no longer be able to embarrass her. In addition, she was aware of feeling angry. On the surface, she was annoyed with her mother for having ignored warnings that her diet and lifestyle would lead to a heart attack; more deeply, however, she was still furious that her mother had forced her as a child to give up a comfortable, happy existence for one fraught with pressure and pain. Vivien's heart attack gave Susan an opportunity to vent some of these feelings in what seemed like an appropriate manner.

Vivien recovered and began to make the changes needed to prolong her life. She lost weight, began to exercise, changed her diet, and stopped smoking. Susan was supportive, but the underlying hostility and emotional estrangement remained. At the beginning of Vivien's recovery, Susan called her mother several times a week. After a while, however, she reverted to the obligatory once-a-week call. Over the next decade, Vivien had two subsequent heart-related illnesses. Each time, Susan rallied around her mother for a while, and then backed away once more.

At age 69, Vivien was diagnosed with cancer. An operation was recommended. Once again, Susan responded as a dutiful daughter. She accompanied her mother to her doctor's appointments and was on hand for the surgery. She appeared to be the model daughter, an example to others of how a loving child should respond to her mother's needs. She even aided her mother in her recovery and insisted on paying a portion of the medical bills not covered by insurance.

All the while, below the surface, Susan continued to feel distant and even hostile. She effectively suppressed such feelings, pushing them aside and acting as if she felt nothing but love and concern. She was, of course, in great emotional turmoil. She loved her mother, but also felt resentment and pain. This state of ambivalence produced stress, anxiety, confusion, guilt, and a variety of intense and conflicting emotions. She diverted herself from these feelings by attending to practical tasks. You see, by this time Susan was not simply plagued with repressed feelings about her childhood only. Her whole evaluative framework had been distorted as a result of her misperceptions about the early changes in her life. She had harbored these inaccuracies, not sharing them with anyone, and thus precluded any chance of resolving her feelings. Vivien's inability to confront her daughter's subsequent behavior left Susan alone in her distortion. To Susan, the world was an unstable place in which safety and security could be wrenched away at any moment; hence, she had a need to control and tried to avoid any conditions under which she might lose it. Her feelings about her mother, because of their intensity and magnitude, were too dangerous to confront, so she suppressed them. But suppression only made them more powerful and thus an even greater threat to her control. Therefore, when faced with a crisis such as her mother's illness, she handled details and avoided feelings, appearing as a model daughter when in fact she was an ambivalent and deeply troubled one.

This pattern repeated a few years later when Vivien had to undergo bypass surgery – a risky procedure for someone so advanced in age. Vivien was afraid that she would not awaken from the surgery. She made a point of saying farewells to her family. She let them know that she loved them and instructed them always to remember that fact. Susan told Vivien that she loved her and believed she would survive. Before the surgery, Susan helped Vivien draw up a living will that stipulated the conditions under which Vivien should not be kept alive by extraordinary means. Once again, Susan focused on an intellectual task in order to prevent being overwhelmed by the painful feelings she held within her. Both mother and daughter were well aware of the tension that overcast their relationship, but neither attempted to deal with it. Vivien, who was never a confrontive individual, chose to focus her energy on surviving the surgery, while Susan, as usual, was content to occupy her mind with practical details.

Vivien survived this medical crisis. Physically, she made a complete recovery. Her mind, however, was never the same. After the surgery, Vivien became prone to periods of confusion and agitation.

Vivien's mind deteriorated markedly in the period following her operation. At times, she would lose her train of thought and forget what she was doing. She might vacuum half of a room and then forget to vacuum the other half, or prepare a roast and place it in the oven, but not remember to turn on the heat. Other times, she became agitated for no apparent reason. Even she could not explain why she was upset. Although she was sometimes lucid and able to carry on logical, insightful conversations, it was clear that her mental functions were deteriorating at a rapid rate. If there was any unfinished business to be done with her, it needed to be attended to quickly.

It was this realization that finally led Susan to seek help. Susan came to my office under the guise of needing support for a short while to get over the stress of her mother's bypass surgery. In her mind, needing support during a crisis was an acceptable reason for seeking professional assistance. On a deeper level, however, Susan was attempting to deal with the lifetime of pain that she had managed to avoid. As soon as she began to speak about her mother, she broke into tears. These were not the tears of someone who had faced a crisis and needed to release tension; these were deep, deep sobs, almost wails of pain. Much of our first session was devoted to this emotional outburst.

At the beginning of the next session, Susan attempted to put a logical explanation on this behavior. She said that the bypass surgery had made her more anxious than she had realized, but she was pleased to discover that she could release her feelings so quickly. She believed that this indicated how strong she was and that her treatment would likely be short-term. Perhaps by force of habit, Susan was using spin control to save face and to keep dangerous emotions at bay. This time, however, her need to express her feelings outweighed her need to feel safe. As soon as I brought the conversation back to an emotional rather than a cognitive level by simply asking how she felt about her mother, Susan again began to sob, with the same intensity as before. This occurred at several more sessions.

Many people would have fled from such intensity and stopped coming to therapy. To Susan's credit, she stuck by her commitment to treatment and found the strength needed to continue. She soon came to realize that her feelings were only in small part about her mother's surgery. More deeply, they were about the pain that she had stored inside for many years – the blow to her self-esteem she had received when her parents changed their lifestyle and the discontinuity and embarrassment she had experienced in high school. Susan was tormented by a deep emotional conflict – she loved and desired nurturance from her mother, but at the same time resented her, for she felt that Vivien had robbed her of a secure, happy childhood and cast her into a milieu that was painful and difficult.

Susan eventually came to understand how her conflicting feelings had affected many of her choices in life. The decision to attend an out-of-town college and law school reflected her desire to escape the anguish she had experienced when with her mother. The decision to move away from Philadelphia was similarly motivated. Living there was stressful, as Vivien would often call and want to get together. To avoid the pain of contact, Susan was creative at offering excuses; but rebuffing her mother only added the pain of guilt, for Susan always felt remorse afterwards. After she and her family left Philadelphia, they returned to see Vivien only once a year. Despite her mother's protests, Susan always insisted on staying at a hotel. When Vivien made her once-a-year trip to see Susan, Susan dutifully threw out the welcome mat; but she avoided spending time with her mother by filling each day of the visit with prescheduled activities.

Susan's conflicts left her in a quandary. She desired a connection to her mother, but avoided contact with her at every juncture, experiencing guilt and confusion as a result. Suppressing her feelings seemed the easiest solution and, over the years, had become a habit. While Susan was a successful attorney, she admitted that her mothering skills and her ability to connect emotionally with others were restricted. Functionally, she did all the right things; internally, there was something missing. What was wrong was that any emotion she experienced tapped into all the powerful feelings she had suppressed. She feared, on some level, being overwhelmed and perhaps destroyed by the intensity of such feelings, so she protected herself by limiting the emotionality of her responses.

Of course, Susan's conflicts also kept her from enjoying the love that Vivien had to offer. Here were two people who loved each other and desired a close relationship, but instead remained distant. Vivien, for her part, deeply regretted her lack of connectedness with Susan. Indeed, she felt closer to her grandchildren than to her daughter. For many years, she wondered what she had done to deserve such aloofness and hostility. She broached the subject with her sisters and her clergyman, but none of them could help her to understand fully or to change the situation. Of course, Vivien appreciated Susan's involvement when she was ill and took it as a sign that her daughter really did love her after all. She told herself that what a person did when the chips were down was what really counted – and Susan had come through unfailingly in such circumstances. But Vivien did not really believe this.

How a person behaves in a crisis is certainly important, but day-to-day encounters are the substance of our lives. Poor Vivien had to contend with the reality that her daughter was there for the short-term emergency, but absent the rest of the time. At some point, she concluded that her daughter's private school and Ivy League education had made her an insensitive snob who was ashamed of her parents.

Vivien was deeply hurt by this realization. She was both saddened and angered by her daughter's behavior. Anger was an uncommon response for Vivien, so it was painful for her to admit that she felt it. More destructively, her daughter's behavior hit at the core of Vivien's own insecurities. Perhaps, she wondered, she had failed as a mother, and her daughter was correct in rejecting her. The circularity of her thinking was clear. If Vivien had done a good job in raising her, Susan would have been a caring, responsive, and involved child; because Susan was distant and hostile, Vivien must have been an incompetent mother.

Consider the significance of this reasoning for Vivien. Being Susan's mother had been the central theme of her life. Vivien believed that the responsibilities of motherhood linked her to her own parents and forebears and to all who would come after in subsequent generations. No other endeavor in her life bore such weight. Here she was, in her final days, in her moments of lucidity, contending with the idea that she had failed. Undoubtedly, the stress and anxiety of this realization contributed to Vivien's decline. True, the ravages of heart disease and cancer were the direct causes of Vivien's death; but her troubled emotional state could only have worsened her physical condition. More importantly, this sense of failure undermined the quality of her life in her final moments, for it prevented her from feeling fulfilled and from having a sense of continuity and realized purpose. In short, it robbed her of contentedness, and thus her life ended sadly, with little resolution.

What resolution there was emanated from the sessions we had in which Susan and Vivien confronted their issues. Once, I saw Vivien alone; once, I saw mother and daughter together. Unfortunately, Vivien died of a stroke upon her return to Philadelphia, a few days after our last meeting. The work we had begun was useful, but ended irrevocably before it was done. Vivien died in emotional distress, and Susan must live with her own pain. Susan continues to work on her issues, but the dimension of working it out with her mother is lost and can never be regained.

Let us look more closely at their all-too-brief treatment. Vivien had come to visit Susan as she periodically did. This time, instead of the usual superficiality and busyness that prevented meaningful contact, Susan had an alternative agenda, for she had come to understand her ambivalence and had begun to feel that it was time not to just explore her feelings, but to confront them as well. She had decided that she would try to discuss her insights with Vivien in a nonthreatening manner. Perhaps she could begin a new relationship with her mother, free of the demons that had haunted her in the past.

When Vivien arrived, however, Susan found herself once again angry and resentful. She told me that on several occasions, as she attempted to speak to Vivien, she became almost tongue-tied. Her mind wanted to follow the plan, but her emotions rebelled against it. Instead of being nonconfrontational, she was short and crisp and negative. Vivien responded defensively, and a cool, tense interchange ensued. Mother and daughter found themselves playing the familiar roles, locked in a dance of destructive predictability, seemingly unable to create a new rhythm that would enable them to step outside of their usual interactive mode. They found themselves, that is, in the same place they had been throughout most of Susan's adult life.

There was a difference, however. Susan's work with me had led to some insight about this very process. This time, even in the throes of such an exchange, she was able to recognize the return of the familiar, unproductive pattern. As a result, rather than becoming caught in its grip, she viewed each interaction with Vivien as an opportunity to handle herself differently. She realized that if she could in some small way depart from the usual pattern, the entire system would necessarily be forced to change.

This, of course, is what might be thought of as the law of interactive systems. A static system remains predictable only so long as no change is introduced. As soon as some aspect of the system changes, a reactive shift occurs in some other part, and this results in more extensive and meaningful change. It is possible to build upon a small shift, viewing it not as a single isolated event, but as the beginning of a series of alterations that, when added together, amount to a significant change in the whole system. Change in itself is neither good nor bad. But change in a static system that is dysfunctional, in a system that produces anguish and disharmony rather than safety and comfort, is always positive. If the change is in the direction of a closer, more harmonious relationship, some would label it good; if it is in the direction of increased conflict and possible dissolution, many would call it bad. In fact, *good* and *bad* are not useful terms here. Any event that produces change in a static, unfulfilling, and dysfunctional relationship is *positive* simply because it forces change. Take, for example, a husband and wife who remain locked in a relational pattern that is stagnant and unfulfilling, but at the same time predictable and safe. If some event occurs that produces an alteration in this pattern, it is positive *regardless of whether or not the marriage survives.* The change is positive if it leads to greater intimacy and fulfillment, but it is also positive if it leads to divorce, for each person is then free to seek a healthier relationship with someone else. Of course, many people will move on to relationships that are just as dysfunctional, repeating the pattern. However, change in the *original* relationship provided an opportunity, whether seized or not, for a different type of pattern to develop.

For Susan, any change meant hope for improvement in her relationship with Vivien. As a result of her insights, Susan was able to reduce the intensity of her negative interaction with her mother. In doing this, she shifted the balance of the old system slightly into a new direction. This new direction allowed Susan to approach each encounter as if it were a new one and, therefore, to tone down her resentment and lessen the level of discord. This was no small feat. Susan had to stop and think about automatic reactions and then override them. Indeed, her attempts at last produced some small but significant changes in the interactive system between mother and daughter. These changes led to a less defensive and less painful interchange, for Vivien seemed to respond intuitively to her daughter's behavior. Eventually, they allowed Susan to tell Vivien that she was in treatment and trying to come to terms with her unhappy feelings toward her mother. This disclosure was truly an amazing event, for it was the first time mother and daughter together acknowledged the fact that a problem existed between them. Because of her efforts, Susan successfully altered their relational pattern and, in doing so, made it possible for them to face the problem together.

The old adage about the whole being greater than the sum of its parts rang true. Together, mother and daughter were more capable of dealing with the problem than either had been alone. To Susan's surprise, Vivien asked how she could help her daughter with her search for meaningful answers. To this end, Susan encouraged Vivien to come in to see me.

Vivien was, in my estimation, a delightfully open woman. In one interview alone, she was able to discuss the problem that existed between her and Susan from her point of view in a direct and forthright manner. She understood that her daughter resented her, but wondered what her crime was, what she had done to create their estrangement. After all, the actions that had destroyed Susan's sense of identity and security had been undertaken for Susan's benefit, and moreover had required much sacrifice on Vivien's part. She was filled with hurt over the distance that had developed between her and Susan, and she recounted how often she had tried to identify the demons that had rendered their relationship so painful. Alas, poor Vivien was faced with trying to solve a riddle with only half of the information necessary to do so; the equation could not balance because her inability to discuss the situation with her daughter left much of the information she needed beyond her grasp. As Vivien related incident after incident, it became clear that even if Susan and she could discuss their differences and have a close, productive relationship for the next few years, those years could never make up for the lifetime of suffering that Vivien had endured. After our meeting, Vivien felt comfortable setting up a session for her daughter and herself to participate together in the long-avoided confrontation.

They both entered the office tentatively and, for an hour and a half, each explained her interpretation of the events of her life. Vivien described how she lay awake at night trying to solve the mystery of her daughter's behavior. Susan described the impact of their changes in lifestyle and her transfer to private school and the resultant cultural discontinuity she had experienced. Each began to see how she had reacted to the other's behavior and how that reaction had contributed to their terrible estrangement, all the while crying tears of joy as well as hurt. Each slowly began to understand the other, to comprehend the missing data needed to make sense of their interactive pattern.

A new relationship had begun that offered the possibility of closeness and intimacy. Susan and Vivien tried desperately to cling to what might now be possible and to step aside from a past they could not change. But the damage had been done. All those years they had remained emotionally distant could never be recovered. No matter how close they now became, no matter how much intimacy they achieved, the inexorable reality was that there would always be decades of missed opportunity and virtually a lifetime of estrangement, and for this there had to be great remorse.

There is no way around such remorse. It must be dealt with directly, in an open though painful manner, for only then can it be resolved and the people involved become free to move ahead with their lives unencumbered. Those who do otherwise remain trapped in a painful landscape. To ward off such pain, they limit their emotional response to life; they will not tap the reservoir of suppressed emotion, because they are afraid they might drown in it.

Clearly, Susan and Vivien had a lot of work yet to do, and many issues yet to resolve. For that day, however, they had done enough. The session ended with tears and hugs. Both women felt a sense of closeness and looked forward to blending together in a new way. They resolved to continue their dialogue by letter and phone and during visits, and perhaps even to seek counseling. Vivien was leaving that very afternoon. The women parted on a high note.

Susan later explained to me how, during the next few days, she often thought about calling Vivien and talking with her at length. However, one of her children had a large science project due that week, and Susan became sidetracked by helping out with it, as well as by the normal responsibilities of her daily routine. One night, she set aside time to call her mother, but when the time came, she was simply too fatigued. She told herself that she would call Vivien on the weekend when she had more time. It is not hard to understand Susan's thinking. Many of us live such busy existences that we find little time or energy for our elderly parents. Many of us live in the illusion that, because our parents have been there all of our lives, they will continue to be there forever; we can call or visit them another time because there will always be another time.

Time runs out, however, and illusion gives way to reality. Four days after Vivien returned home, she had a stroke. Although life support kept her body alive, her mind had died. Susan would never get to make that call. Sadly, one moment of connectedness was all there would be. Mother and daughter would forever be unable to take their new understanding any further. Susan flew to Philadelphia and stood holding Vivien's hand as the life support systems were shut off and Vivien's heart gradually slowed down and stopped, her body finally synchronizing with her already dead mind. Susan remembers standing by the grave alone, tormented with guilt that she had not done all or even some of what she should have done for her mother. She regretted that she had not made her mother's life easier, that she had not shouldered some of her financial burdens, that she had not sent her on trips to places she had always dreamed of going – all of which were well within her power. Worse, she was painfully aware that she had not fulfilled even the most basic duties of a daughter. She had turned away from her mother whenever she had been presented with the opportunity to turn toward her, time and time again. Sadly, she would she never get the chance to make amends.

In Vivien's last days, Susan had worked hard to move in the direction of reconciliation. It was not completely a case of too little too late, for Vivien died with a sense of being loved by her daughter and with considerable understanding of their estrangement. However, Susan was left to deal not only with her remorse for all the years before, but also with the loss of hope for a new beginning, as there can be no such beginning any longer.

Susan is not a villain, not a bad person. Rather, she is someone who allowed her feelings of ambivalence to cloud her judgment and to affect her life in a negative way. If she is guilty of one thing, it is of allowing the years to pass by in silence and resentment rather than trying to improve the relationship. Vivien in her own limited way made attempts to change the interactive pattern with her daughter, but Susan either missed the attempts or chose to reject them and remained, instead, locked into her ambivalence. Now, she must work to reach a level of resolution that will allow her some peace of mind. One day, she may get beyond her remorse and her guilt. She continues to work toward this end, and I have hope that she can reach it, but how far she can go is still an open question that only time can answer.

This brings us to the end of the tale of Vivien and Susan. Let us now draw some universal lessons from the details of their experiences.

Several themes come to mind. First and foremost, we have a responsibility to relate to and care for our aged parents, regardless of the difficulties that might have arisen over the years. This responsibility is one many adult children evade for a variety of reasons. Some make a deliberate choice based on how they were treated as children. For example, some refuse to care for a parent who physically, sexually, or verbally abused them. This sort of catastrophic sequence is relatively uncommon, however. In the majority of situations, it is the adult child's *unresolved emotional misunderstanding* that leads to a failure to act on behalf of an aging parent, as we have seen in the case of Susan and Vivien.

Being wrapped up in our own lives, taking care of our own children and financial burdens, can lead to a general inability to recognize our parents' needs, or to a selective perception that justifies our inaction. *Selective perception* means recognizing only what fits an agenda and virtually ignoring other, perhaps significant, data. For example, the parent may show signs of loneliness, depression, and withdrawal, but the child observes only that the parent leads a quiet existence and is content with his privacy. In this case, the child chooses to see only enough information to justify a lack of involvement on his part.

Rationalization and denial are other mechanisms that people use to justify a failure to care for their aging parents. I am reminded of a man who told me that, despite his own wishes to the contrary, he found it necessary to place his father in an elder care home due to his father's poor health and frailty. This did not seem unreasonable to me. However, when I had occasion to visit the father some weeks later, I came to see a completely different picture. In the course of our conversation, it became clear that the father was of sound mind and body and that his admission to the home was, in fact, questionable. The father explained that his son had always assured him that if living alone became too difficult, he could move in with the son. However, what actually occurred was quite different and even diabolical. Each time the son came to visit, he pointed out how ill-kept the father's house and yard were, and how difficult it was for him to find time to come over and help his father with the chores. Since getting groceries, cooking meals, and other daily tasks were becoming more difficult for the father, after a while he accepted his son's offer. He sold his house and, as part of the arrangement, gave his son power of attorney and guardianship of his funds. As soon as the papers were signed, the son took all of his father's funds. He then stated that his father probably should not live with him after all, and promptly placed the old man in an elder care home that was comfortable, but far from extravagant, and, indeed, somewhat cheap. Thus was the father manipulated into an inappropriate situation, and, like many older people, he was too proud to confront his son. Moreover, he feared that if he did, he might be cast out from even this home and lose the sporadic visits from his grandchildren. So he remained silent but filled with anger and pain, for he had trusted in his son and been swindled by him.

I felt that it was my responsibility to discuss this with the son. I did so tactfully, only to discover that the son had completely rationalized his actions. He explained how he had originally worried about his father's not being able to manage his life and cited instances of older people setting their houses on fire and perishing. He also mentioned that it was common for the elderly to restrict their diets and lose weight to the point of starvation. And there were so many con artists trying to dupe older people out of their money! All of this led him to the idea of getting his father to move in with him. However, after his father's house was sold, he realized how confusing it might be for an aged person at his home, what with the kids coming in and out and the pets and toys that might be tripped over. There was also the risk of the old fellow setting the house on fire. Besides, the house had two stories and there was no way his father could deal with the stairs. In time, living there could prove dangerous. It made perfect sense to place his father in a safe environment with people his own age and with staff that could care for him. He realized that his father was not entirely happy with this arrangement, but he was sure the old man would do well after a period of adjustment.

All of this made sense on the surface, except that I knew the father, and I was aware that his level of functioning was considerably higher than the son described. It was clear, however, that the son believed what he was saying. He had rationalized the facts so that they came out the way he wanted. This line of thinking had allowed him to get most of his father's assets, to protect his inheritance from being used up on his father's needs, to tuck the old man away, and to excuse himself from all responsibility except the occasional visit. Meanwhile, the son could tell himself and everyone else that he had acted in his father's best interest! My attempts over time to convince him of his mistake proved fruitless and led to some resentment towards me. Some months later, I was saddened to hear that the father had committed suicide, by letting himself waste away. The poor man must have realized that his son's wish was to get rid of him. He must have felt that being manipulated and exploited by his own flesh and blood was too painful to live with and, in a last angry action, rejected life and ended his pain.

This history is an extreme. It does illustrate, however, how a person can rationalize away the facts and make crucial decisions based on selectively perceived data. We must learn from such an example and work toward avoiding these mechanisms, even in their subtlest forms, in our own lives.

Of course, pride in older people can cause them to *present* selective information as well. It was pride that led the old gentleman to mask his despair over his son's actions, with catastrophic results. Pride kept Vivien from confronting the situation with her daughter and consigned her to languish in emotional pain. Pride, selective perception, rationalization, misunderstandings perhaps dating back to childhood – all of these can lead adult children to miss opportunities to act on their aging parents' behalf, or even lead them to act in ways that are deleterious to them.

It is very important to look at the sort of relationship you have with your aged parent. Consider how it operates. Do you communicate well or are there barriers? If there are barriers, from where do they stem? Are you stuck in an unproductive and unfulfilling interactive pattern? What steps can you take to change that pattern? Do not be passive, like Susan and Vivien. Act now to understand and to get past whatever hinders you. To hesitate is to risk losing years of what could be more meaningful connectedness. And the consequences can be tragic, as we have seen.

Recently, a new kind of service has arisen that can be of invaluable assistance in caring for aged parents. This service involves a geriatric specialist who meets with the parents and objectively evaluates their circumstances along a number of dimensions. The specialist looks at the parents' level of functioning and quality of life, and then makes recommendations about what is available to enhance their situation. A comprehensive evaluation of this kind is not costly, and can be helpful in many ways. First, it can function as an objective check on misperceptions and denials, whether they emanate from the children or the parents. Second, it can help children who live in a different locale to monitor their parents when it is not possible for the children themselves to visit. Third, it can provide a second opinion or clarification to assure the children that they are doing all they can to care for their parents. Finally, such a service has access to a wide variety of resources, some of which may be difficult for the children to discover on their own.

Of course, such specialists can only broadly assess the conditions in which your parents live. They may miss subtle conditions, especially those of an emotional nature. Do not expect this kind of consultant to make an assessment of your parents' emotional state unless it is obvious that they are significantly depressed or anxious. This task is best accomplished by someone who knows your parents well, someone who is aware of their personalities and can pick up on subtle changes and shifts in mood. Remember that it is not uncommon for elderly people to hide their feelings and deficiencies and to be overly accommodating. It is also easy for the adult children to believe what is on the surface and not seek to go more deeply. When our lives are busy, it suits our convenience not to recognize difficulties, unless they are urgent. If an aged parent falls and is injured, we are forced to take action. If the injury is of an emotional nature, however, and does not require immediate intervention, we find it easy to overlook. This is not because we are callous people. Rather, it is because we are human and another set of demands is, at times, unpleasant to contemplate. Besides, on a deeper level, most of us do not want to acknowledge that the once vibrant person who cared for us is now in need of our care.

We must give up the illusion of having strong, protective, nurturing parents; we must accept the fact that we as adults are now the caretakers, not only of our children, but also of our aged parents. In instances where parents have provided a positive experience, this illusion is naturally very hard to give up. When the experience has been less than positive, paradoxically, the pull to keep the illusion is even stronger, because giving it up means facing the fact that there is no hope of ever receiving such nurturance.

It is important to consider not just the basic conditions and circumstances in our aged parents' lives, but also the *quality* of their lives. Doing this requires sensitivity, emotional energy, and a considerable expenditure of time; but the results can be most rewarding. We need to help our aged parents maximize this stage of their lives, and this goes beyond mere functional caretaking. Moreover, as we have learned from the story of Susan and Vivien, trying to resolve old issues that create distance is most important, for such resolution can enrich communication and help an aged parent not just to survive, but to flourish.

Such resolution benefits the adult children as well. When we seek to improve our relations with our aged parents, we confront issues that might otherwise remain lurking in our psyches, robbing us of energy and clouding our judgment. In addition, we set the example for the next generation. How will our children learn about their responsibilities to us as aged parents if we do not provide them with a model? How will they resolve their issues with us if we do not show them how? As we take care of our aged parents, our children learn how to care for us, not merely in the physical sense, though this is important, but in the emotional sense as well. If we demonstrate concern and sensitivity, we teach our children to do the same.

Do not be like Susan. Do not hesitate to deal with the difficulties in your relationship with your aging parents, or you will one day find yourself alone in your grief and remorse, adapting to an unrequited emotional connection. *Act now,* so that you may add meaning and joy to your life, as well as to the lives of your aged parents and your children.

My mother was a good and loving person. While many would envy this, and rightfully so, there was an aspect of my mother's gentleness that created turmoil in my relationship with her, until we had the insight and fortitude to confront it and work it out. For many years, my mother tended to overprotect me. She protected my brothers as well, but not with nearly the intensity she did me. As a child, I believed that she behaved in this way because I was less competent than my brothers and peers. For example, no matter where I was going or how early I would be coming home, my mother always warned me about what could go wrong. Then, she waited up for me, as if to say she believed I would get into trouble and need her help. One time, I had a date with a girl in Brooklyn, which was quite a trip from our home in the Bronx. Before I left, my mother voiced a number of her concerns. She worried that I had to travel a long distance on the subway and that anything could happen on such a trip, especially on the way home late at night. Why didn't I just find a nice girl in the immediate neighborhood and skip the trip? She gave me extra money to take a taxi. All of this was done in a supportive manner. However, because she never identified specific concerns, but instead vaguely alluded to the worst possibilities, it was left for me to fill in the substance of her fears on the long trip to Brooklyn. I concluded that she did not believe I was capable of managing the situation. This, of course, undermined my self-confidence, and I began to feel I was inadequate. Literally, she had planted her fears into my sensibility. She did not do this maliciously; nevertheless, her cautions made me insecure.

This happened many times in the course of my childhood, in a thousand different ways. "If you play ball, be careful, or you will break a leg." "If you go out in the cold, you might catch pneumonia." "Don't drink alcohol, or you will lose control." These were the echoes of her worries that I had to face. Initially, I felt that my mother must have had good reason to lack confidence in me. Later, I realized that she was the one with the problem, not me; but for years this realization never really took, and I remained shy and insecure. As an emerging adult in college, when I began to function completely on my own, I started to wonder why my mother felt the way she did. Her idea of me did not coincide with my own. Finally, I sat down with her and told her what I had experienced. She was dumbfounded. She said that she had complete confidence in me and always had. She never intended to impart doubts to me, but only to caution me about those things that made her afraid. As we talked, we looked back, and soon a theme emerged which made sense to both of us. My mother had lost two children before I was born, and I was born prematurely. Thus, my mother was doubly aware that she might lose me. As a result, she held back on bonding with me; then, when it became apparent that I would survive, she overbonded. I became the child she was afraid she would lose. She felt an intense need to make sure that I was protected, so she found herself cautioning me more frequently than she did my siblings.

For years, we never discussed this issue. Instead, it remained as a barrier which impeded our communication, though not one that prevented us from being close in other ways. Once we talked about it and understood the process, however, we were able to work together to overcome it. For example, if I my mother cautioned me when I was going somewhere, instead of getting upset, I would say something like, "You know, mother, I'm not your premature little baby any longer," and she would laugh and exclaim how I had certainly grown into a six-foot-tall premature baby, or some such comment. What had existed as a tension was now transformed into a joke, because we had talked about it. I was amazed how free I felt realizing that she did, in fact, have confidence in me. She felt free because she was no longer harboring her old fears about losing me. Talking our difficulty through had relieved a strain from both of us, and opened up a dialogue that continued for many years.

Our relationship had grown and progressed in many ways, but it had stagnated in this one regard, causing misunderstanding and confusion. Resolution paved the way for even more open communication. Finally, I could see my mother's gentleness clearly, without worrying that she doubted my ability. My mother had learned to encounter her most disturbing fears, to confront them and release the energy she had devoted to protecting herself from them — a process which made her at once more relaxed and energetic. Now that the strain between us was gone, the quality of both of our emotional lives was significantly improved.

How fortunate I was to have had a mother who was willing to work with me to strengthen and enhance our relationship in this way! It took courage and a willingness to extend herself beyond her limits, to grow emotionally even at an advanced age.

CHAPTER THREE

TOUGH CHOICES,
CONFLICTING FEELINGS

This chapter deals with decisions many readers will be forced to face: decisions about when an aged parent should move into your home or into a nursing home or other care facility. In the previous chapter, we looked at an adult child who felt ambivalently about helping her aged parent because of the painful unresolved issues between them. In this chapter, we will examine making decisions which, even when we feel positively about our aged parents, involve us in conflicted and ambivalent emotions.

First of all, it can be difficult to accept the reality that our aged parents need our help. It is hard to let go of the image of our parents as strong and powerful caregivers. As children, we depended on them to nurture and protect us, to give us food and shelter, and, whenever we felt like the world was closing in on us, to intervene and come to our aid. As young adults, we depended on them for advice and support. Many of us also depended on them for financial help, for assistance with school tuition or with the downpayment for our first house or car. As life progressed, our parents were there for our weddings and the births of our children, and they held our hands when adversity struck. Because we have come to rely on our parents, we tend to live in the illusion that they will always be there. As our parents age and decline, however, we are forced to realize that this illusion can no longer be maintained, that it is now our responsibility to care for them as they have cared for us. We must face this reality: the roles have reversed.

We are, of course, speaking of parents and children who have enough of a bond that both wish to engage in an ongoing relationship. In one view, however, parents are simply the people who conceived and raised us, and nowhere is it written that we must relate to them beyond our childhood years. In some instances, the parent-child relationship was so traumatic that there is a desire to make a clean break. I am reminded of a situation I encountered some years back. A patient of mine, Marjorie, wished to sever all ties with her alcoholic father, who had terrorized her as a child. She had witnessed physical abuse and grown up in an environment in which she never knew when explosive, violent behavior might erupt. After her father abandoned the family when she was seven years old, Marjorie felt relief. He did not reenter her life until many years later, when she was an adult with a family of her own. Out of the blue, he phoned Marjorie and told her he wanted to reestablish their relationship. Lured by the prospect of getting some of the parental attention she had been deprived of for so many years, Marjorie warily agreed to meet him for lunch. To her disgust, she discovered not only that he still drank heavily, but that he wanted to exploit her for financial help! Naturally, Marjorie felt that her father was set to abuse her again. She broke off all contact and was successful in working out her residual feelings in therapy. She has since moved on with her life.

This is not the sort of relationship we are discussing here. Rather, we are concerned with the much more common relationship where there is enough of an emotional bond that the adult child is willing to be involved in his aged parent's life and needs. This does not mean that all is perfect between them. Conflicts and misunderstandings, and at times negative feelings, are bound to occur. However, the dominant features are loyalty and a desire to participate in decision-making. In short, there is love.

But it is this very love that makes decisions so difficult for the adult child to face. Making decisions requires the child to identify the point at which the parent can no longer be trusted to live on his own. This means that the child must relinquish his illusion that his parent is all-powerful and recognize the weakening effects of the aging process. Such a shift in perception is difficult enough, but it is even more difficult when the parent does not agree with the child's assessment and denies or tries to cover up his decline. In such cases, the child becomes reluctant to speak up for fear of injuring the parent's pride. Both parent and child must engage in a process of negotiation and creative problem-solving in order to handle the situation delicately and positively. In many cases, the burden falls upon the child to initiate this process.

Decision-making is further complicated when coming to an agreement on the facts seems impossible. For example, the adult child may observe that his aged parent is reluctant to leave the house for fear of getting lost. Perhaps the parent is not eating enough food because he is afraid to go to the store. But the aged parent may offer a different perception: he prefers the quiet comforts of home over the noise and commotion outdoors; he cooks only when he is hungry, and, because he is less active, he is not as hungry as he used to be.

Such differences in perception lead to very different conclusions and very complex interactions. The adult child may feel that there is a need for part-time supervision, while the aged parent may dismiss the child's concern as overreactive. In extreme instances, the aged parent may feel insulted and become angry and defensive, and it is not uncommon for an adult child confronted with such a response to feel guilty and to become defensive and angry as well. Such negative interactions can lead to serious breaches in the relationship and even to a complete break. If the relationship continues, further friction is usually avoided, often with dire consequences. The adult child may refrain from bringing up important observations for fear of starting another fight, and the aged parent may keep fears and anxieties to himself for the same reason. In some cases, parent and child stay in a holding pattern until some disaster occurs and the parent is so incapacitated that legal action is necessary; in such circumstances, the child ends up forcing a solution on the parent in which the parent has had no say.

Obviously, it is best to preclude such situations. Child and parent must take care to focus their interaction around the reality of reduced functioning. While this is not an easy thing to pull off, there is a better chance of succeeding if possible pitfalls can be anticipated. The stories in this chapter will provide insight into the nuances of such exchanges and offer some creative and pragmatic responses to the problems that can arise. Today in this country, we are fortunate to have a variety of support systems for the elderly, ranging from supplementary to total care; let us examine the opportunities they afford at each stage of our aged parents' decline.

I recall a man in his eighties who was reasonably functional, but had trouble adjusting to the absence of his wife, whom he had recently lost. Because his wife had always taken care of the housework, he had never cooked, cleaned, or done laundry. Nevertheless, he had a fierce resolve to remain in his apartment and to live on his own. Initially, his children helped him, but they were not always available when needed, since they lived in other parts of the state. One day, a bulb blew out in the chandelier above their father's favorite chair, where he liked to sit and read every evening. It was not practicable for the children to travel to their father's apartment until the weekend, so for several days his routine was disrupted. During this time, the children were afraid that, in frustration, their father would attempt to change the bulb himself and fall off the ladder and get injured.

Such situations naturally arise, and it is best to be prepared for them. One good idea is for the aged parent living on his own to keep a list of things he has questions about so that they can be addressed on the next visit. Another is for the adult child regularly to inspect the parent's home looking for things to do and catching problems before they arise. But no matter how well organized their system is, parent and child cannot foresee everything. It is best, then, in situations such as this, to find someone living nearby whom the aged parent can ask for assistance.

This family recognized the need for such a person and came up with a perfectly workable solution. Living in the father's apartment building was a middle-aged woman whom the family had known for years. She had a warm feeling for the father, so it was simply a matter of requesting that she keep an eye on him. The adult children offered to pay her, but she refused. Instead, an unspoken bargain was reached: they would provide her with any professional services she needed for which they were qualified. She, being a caring and responsible person, checked on the father every day. She often brought him food and advised him on how to cook his own meals. If he had trouble doing the laundry, she helped. When a light bulb burned out, she changed it. She even unclogged a drain.

Here was someone on the scene who could take care of the aged parent when the adult children were not readily available. In effect, this arrangement allowed the parent to live independently and still have the minimal intervention he required. If you find yourself faced with similar concerns, you should consider such a solution. If your parent has resided in a particular building or neighborhood for a long period, it may be possible to locate a friendly neighbor who is willing to assume an intercessory role. It also may be possible to hire someone to fill this need, and local churches and synagogues can direct you to people who are responsible and willing.

As our aged parents require more help, other plans must be adopted. One option is to hire a professional specializing in gerontology to do a needs assessment followed by an ongoing review, so that it is possible to stay on top of the parent's increasing need for assistance. Such professionals can direct you to resources that may be useful, including organizations that bring regular dinners to the elderly and home health services that provide aides to administer medication to or help bathe the infirm.

Another creative solution is to hire a roommate. Many college students who are working their way through school will look favorably on an arrangement that provides them with room and board in exchange for basic minimal caring for an elderly person. These young people, of course, are not trained to handle significant medical needs, but they can do a lot to make an aged parent's life safer, easier, and even richer.

Recently, I came across an elderly woman who for three years had been living with a young female graduate student in social work. The adult children, all sons, lived in nearby cities. This student had been hired to provide for the increasing needs of the parent, receiving room and board in exchange for care. The young woman cooked, helped buy food, did some cleaning, arranged for yard work, did laundry, reminded the elderly woman when her medication needed to be taken, and helped her get to appointments at the dentist or doctor or hairdresser. She had taken the job as a junior in college, planning only to continue until she graduated. Soon, however, the job came to mean something more to her, and she changed her plans so she could keep it.

This young woman had been close to her grandmother as a child, but her grandmother had died when she was nine years old after a long struggle with cancer. The experience of watching a person she dearly loved deteriorate and ultimately die strongly affected her. She felt that she would have done anything to make her grandmother well again. She remembers praying over and over each night for God to provide a miracle so her grandmother could live. She also remembers feeling guilty after her grandmother died because she had been ineffectual in saving her. Eventually, she came to realize that the longing of a child is not enough to cure a terrible disease. Emotionally, however, she continued to feel the loss as well as the remorse. On many occasions, she fantasized about what life might have been like if her grandmother had lived, about the guidance and wisdom and love her grandmother would have given her.

When the young student took the job, she saw it simply as a logical way to get through school. In time, however, she and her elderly roommate became very close. In fact, she now recognizes that this woman became a surrogate grandparent, someone who could provide what she had longed to receive from her own grandmother. The young student found a healthy way to compensate for her loss, at the same time creating an excellent situation for her elderly roommate. Not only did the older woman have help dealing with her chores and responsibilities, but additionally she had gained a friend and, in a sense, a surrogate daughter. These two developed a deep, abiding love for each other. The intertwining of their needs was mutually beneficial: the elderly woman, who had only sons, now had a daughter, and the young student found the grandmother she had lost.

The elderly woman's sons did not miss the significance of this development. They did not become jealous; instead, they recognized the value of their mother's new friendship, and treated the young woman as a member of the family. They also were well aware that their own lives had become considerably less complicated. Thus, when the young woman decided to stay in the same city, they even decided to help her pay for graduate school. In effect, this was a win–win–win situation. The young woman won because she was able to compensate for a loss in her life while continuing her education. The aged parent won because she now had a loving "daughter" who helped her in her daily life. The adult children won because they could take care of their mother's needs in a way that was meaningful and caring, but only minimally disruptive to their lives.

Of course, not all such situations work out so successfully. In some instances, the care may be perfunctory and uninvolved, and it may become necessary to fire the roommate and look for a better match. Remember that not all people get along with each other. The young woman in the example above could just as easily have experienced the growing relationship with the elderly woman as negative, since it might have activated painful feelings of unresolved guilt about her own grandmother. Be wise and look not only to the concrete needs of your aged parent; try to see beyond practical considerations into the realm of emotionality. The personal relationship that develops in such an arrangement is the critical factor in the success or failure of the whole enterprise.

While covering our aged parents' basic requirements is necessary, it is always more beneficial to do so in a way that promotes emotional well-being and connectedness. *We must be sensitive as well as practical, for attending to the emotional side of things could assure that our aged parents not only function, but thrive.* This is a goal worth striving for and one that can be achieved if we consciously define it as the outcome we desire. Do not be lulled into thinking that attending to mundane tasks is enough. We all have emotional needs, and elderly people have emotional needs as complex as those of younger adults. It is important that we recognize this reality and make a real effort to respond to it with sensitivity and care.

We have explored some of the considerations and options that arise when an aged parent is living independently and begins to have a growing need for support and intervention. The next step toward increased care and supervision is the older adult apartment complex or senior citizens' retirement community, facilities which afford aged parents as much autonomy as they are capable of handling.

In some areas, a sprawling facility of this type constitutes a mega-lopolis for the elderly. Florida's Century Village and Arizona's Sun City are literally cities within cities that offer a variety of services, stores, and recreational activities such as golf, tennis, and swimming pools on their premises. More commonly, facilities of this type rely on the services available within the local community. In all such facilities, large or small, the elderly tenants rent apartments and live on their own, but they are checked on regularly by staff. In addition, each apartment is equipped with an emergency call system, so help is easily summoned when needed. The collective nature of such a place allows for certain conveniences. For example, elderly tenants can opt for meals in a common dining area if they do not wish to cook for themselves, and a recreation center offers social activities such as concerts and lectures. Many facilities provide immunizations and nutritional advice on the premises along with a variety of other services, including professional intervention. If a resident dies, a social worker may be assigned to meet with close friends to help them deal with their loss. Many of these places also have a capacity for in-house care and supervision. If a resident has foot surgery, for example, and cannot get around for a while, a service that cleans, cooks, and helps with various chores is available. Some facilities include a convalescent center that provides nursing home-type care on a temporary or permanent basis. Usually, the convalescent center is affiliated with a hospital, so that patients may go there directly from the hospital to recuperate and never be more than a block away from their friends. Because staying in a familiar setting is especially important and helpful to aged couples, such a comprehensive facility is especially attractive for them.

I am reminded of an elderly couple I once knew. They had been married for over 50 years, and their children were all living in different parts of the country. Marvin had been a professor of horticulture for a local university, and Elaine had been a traditional housewife. Though both had enjoyed good health throughout their lives, the physical labor involved in maintaining their house had become too burdensome. Marvin and Elaine decided to make the transition into an old age complex, and rented an apartment in a federally subsidized facility. Their new apartment, while not spacious, was adequate, with two bedrooms, a living room, and a large eat-in kitchen. They set up the extra bedroom as a study.

It was very difficult for Marvin and Elaine to give up the home they had lived in for over 40 years, the home where their children had been born and raised. It was even more difficult to part with treasured possessions and familiar articles and furniture that would not fit into their reduced living space. Some things were given to their children, and others were donated to charities or sold at garage sales. There was some satisfaction in knowing that their memorabilia would be useful to those in need and to the young families who bought their things. Those items they simply could not part with were placed in storage.

We must recognize that moving into a new home will not be easy for our aged parents. They may plan the move long in advance, and stoically accept it as a necessity, but it will take time for them to adjust emotionally to the changes and losses involved. People become attached to possessions and places and to the memories that they associate with them. We must recognize this and help our aged parents deal with the pain and sadness of letting go. We should encourage them to talk about the move, to cry and be sad if that is what they feel. Telling stories about objects to be left behind can stimulate intense feelings our parents need to express. Do not be afraid of this intensity. Remember, our parents are dealing with a lifetime of attachment, and this is no small matter. If you hear yourself saying things like "Don't cry" or "You will be fine," then you are making a big mistake. *Feeling strong emotions at such a time is normal and appropriate, and expressing them should be encouraged.*

Because Marvin and Elaine went through the transition together, they had the advantage of being able to share their feelings. Single elderly people are not so lucky, and may need to be drawn out. Having friends already in the complex helps, and frequent visits before the move can ease the transition. At many facilities, there is a social worker on staff who can provide support. Again, the point is to recognize that transition issues exist and to figure out how best to respond to them. Do not be afraid to seek professional counsel; sometimes, it is useful to bounce your concerns off a neutral party. A therapist can meet with your parent alone, or meet with you to deal with issues of your own arising from your parent's move, or help you and your parent to problem-solve together. Whatever your approach, consider allowing the process to continue throughout the move and adjustment period, or until it is clear that your parent has fully settled in.

Marvin and Elaine had each other for support, and this eased their situation significantly. Because they had shared so many memories and feelings as they sorted through their old belongings, they were able to begin their new life with optimism and a sense of adventure. They settled into their new surroundings quickly. They discovered that two of Marvin's colleagues from the university resided in the same complex, and they scheduled a regular bridge night with this couple. They made many new friends, too, and developed a social life more active than the one they had enjoyed before! They used the transportation the complex provided to go to malls and movies; they went out to dinner regularly. They attended lectures and other social events at the recreation center. Elaine especially looked forward to the concerts given periodically by the orchestra from a local middle school; she loved talking to the children afterwards when refreshments were served. Marvin and Elaine even located a special area on the grounds where they were allowed to plant their own garden, for both were gardening enthusiasts.

It took about eight months for Marvin and Elaine to feel completely at home. This is by no means a long time in such transitions. Remember, these two had each other for support, and both were very positive and adaptive. Your aged parents may take longer to adjust and may need extensive support from you. If they seem to be adjusting, probe deeper to make sure. Your parents may be putting on a good front for you. Assume that they are experiencing at least a few difficulties, and encourage them to voice their worries and concerns.

Just as Marvin and Elaine were settling in and feeling as if their new life could be rewarding, tragedy struck – Marvin had a stroke and was incapacitated. At first, he could not move much on his left side, his speech was impaired, and it seemed that he had suffered some cognitive damage. In time, however, his speech cleared and, with rehabilitation, he regained a good deal of the movement on his left side.

Marvin, of course, had to be treated in a hospital; for a number of weeks, he remained there for care and rehabilitation. He was then transferred to the facility's nursing home unit. Fortunately, the complex Marvin and Elaine lived in offered a wide continuum of care. The nursing home was on the premises, and the hospital was across the street. This made it possible for Elaine not only to see Marvin every day, but also to be an active member of the team of doctors, nurses, and rehabilitation specialists who worked to help Marvin improve. When a speech therapist prescribed certain exercises for Marvin, Elaine learned how to do them too, so that she could work with her husband. Elaine knew exactly what Marvin's goals were in physical therapy, and she was present to encourage him throughout the process. Elaine joined Marvin in counseling and even attended additional sessions on her own.

When a functioning person is suddenly incapacitated, and an extended period of time must pass before the level of recovery can be determined, a number of psychological factors come into play. After a stroke, for example, loss of sensation and mobility can cause great frustration, and that frustration can turn to anger and depression. Thus, it is not uncommon for stroke victims to weep over their misfortune. Consider

Marvin's predicament. There he was, a professor who had prided himself on his ability to lecture and to write about a variety of subjects, suddenly and without warning unable to speak intelligibly, limited to grunts and facial grimaces. His need to express his feelings is paramount; he is frightened, angry, desperate, and resentful – yet he is incapable of speech. Add to this the fact that no one can assure him that he will ever recover from the catastrophe. His only way of expressing his feelings is by acting out or crying. Anger and tears become his central mode of communication.

I am reminded of an Edgar Allan Poe story in which the central character is in a vegetative physical state resembling death. People around him assume that he is dead, but in fact he is merely under the influence of a drug that simulates death. His thinking is clear and lucid, but his body remains unresponsive. He is unable to express himself to those around him who, believing he is dead, proceed to bury him. The terror and frustration of this character resemble the feelings of a stroke victim who cannot communicate, who is unable to show his mental acuity, who is trapped in his body with no, or few, means of expressing his wishes, his misery, or his fears.

Marvin was fortunate that Elaine was nearby and able to participate in his treatment, for her daily presence did much to help him through his frustration and distress. Because their apartment was so close to the hospital and the convalescent center, Elaine could see Marvin every day and be included in all aspects of his recovery process. Elaine also benefitted from the setup at the facility. She was surrounded by friends and staff members who were available to attend to her emotional as well as her practical needs. She did not have to clean or cook, she was able to talk about her shock and her worries, and she could depend on the routines of the complex to help her deal with the overwhelming nature of her new predicament.

Over a period of months, Marvin recovered significantly, but not completely. There was no evidence of brain damage. While still in the hospital, he began to be able to speak, though his speech was slurred. He continued his recovery in the facility's nursing home. Eventually, he was able to return to his apartment. He continued to have slight paralysis of his left side and slurred speech. Nevertheless, because of the level of care and assistance he received, he was able to resume a full and rewarding life. Unfortunately, about one year after returning to his apartment, Marvin had another more massive stroke, and this time recovery was not possible. He languished for some months in the nursing home, where his wife visited several hours each day, often reading to him, but Marvin eventually passed away.

When Marvin died, Elaine once again had a support system at her disposal. Friends, of course, were there to console her, and facility staff helped with the funeral arrangements. More importantly, counseling services were available to help Elaine through her loss, for she initially was angry that Marvin's body had killed him, and soon became deeply depressed. When Elaine emerged from this phase, she again benefitted from the environment in which she lived. Her proximity to neighbors, friends, and social activities, coupled with the helpfulness of the staff, facilitated her adjustment to life without Marvin, and she eventually resolved her grief and resumed a full life.

In fact, when I last called her to see about going out to lunch or dinner, she had to schedule me three weeks ahead to fit me into her activities! She was going to the theater and concerts; she did volunteer work at the neighboring hospital; she played bridge and was taking some classes. All this, plus her gardening and other pastimes at the complex, kept her life busy, active, and rewarding. She also mentioned that several men at the complex were showing her a lot of attention. In spite of her changed circumstances, Elaine had adjusted and gone on with her life – a positive outcome in which her environment played a major part.

The complex where Marvin and Elaine resided must be looked upon as exceptional, for it is rare to find such a wide continuum of care in one package. Nevertheless, such a facility may be located within the community where your elderly parents reside.

Many facilities do not offer all levels of care, or are affiliated with nursing homes and hospitals that are at other locations. Some do not have any affiliations. But even the smallest complex usually has at least one staff member, such as a nursing home placement specialist or social worker, who has the knowledge and resources to help you place your parent when more extensive care or hospitalization is needed. Distance between services presents a logistical problem that Marvin and Elaine did not have to encounter; but this, too, can be overcome.

Whatever the care options in your parents' area, you should investigate them long before they are needed. Waiting until there is a crisis can lead to hasty, poorly thought out solutions. Begin looking now, when your elderly parents are not in need and can be involved in the investigation. I urge you to preselect a facility well in advance. Visit and participate in activities at the most reasonable facilities in order to gain information about them and make an informed choice. Do not be afraid to interview residents and inquire about all of the concerns you and your parents may have. It is useful to brainstorm and generate a list of questions, so that you are prepared to cover a wide range of topics. Try to find a former neighbor or church or synagogue member who currently resides at any facility that you are seriously considering; an "insider" can be an invaluable source of information.

The time to begin this process is *now*, when you can investigate carefully and thoroughly, without pressure. Moreover, many care facilities have long waiting lists, some as long as one or two years. It is important to get on such lists *now*, so that when the time comes, there is a place for your parents in the facility of their choice. Even facilities that offer a continuum of care may require incoming clients to meet initial criteria, such as the ability to be ambulatory or to care for themselves. Such facilities may decline to admit a person who cannot meet their criteria, and this too must be considered ahead of time. For all these reasons, *act now*. Dialogue with your aged parents and begin to search for a good fit.

Let us now turn to a story that illustrates this point.

Betty did not age well. She had a hip replacement, arthritis, a number of heart attacks, brain damage from strokes, and early stage Alzheimer's disease. By the time she was 82, it was clear that she required full-time supervision. Her husband Arthur, however, could not bear to be separated from her or to relinquish responsibility for her care. After all, Betty had been a loving and devoted wife; she had made many sacrifices for Arthur over the years, and Arthur was deeply grateful.

Betty had always been an independent, strong-minded person. While other women felt pressured to find husbands who made a comfortable living, Betty pursued her own career. Though she had many suitors and several proposals, she vowed to remain single until she found her soul mate, a man who shared her views and beliefs as well as her love for the arts. Betty was 35 when she met and married Arthur.

Arthur was not the kind of man that Betty's peers would consider a "good catch." He was a painter, and he did not care about money. Betty and Arthur fell in love because they shared many intellectual interests, and because Betty believed in Arthur's talent. More than anything, Betty wanted Arthur to pursue his artistic vision unencumbered by practical concerns and without feeling pressured by art world fads. She continued to pursue her own career after they married, so that Arthur could paint full-time without worrying about their finances.

Betty and Arthur had one child. Six months after Prudence was born, Betty returned to work. When Prudence was an infant, Arthur took her with him to the studio each day. When Prudence began to go to school, Arthur would drop her off and pick her up. Prudence liked to watch her father paint. Every once in a while, she would pose for him. Sometimes, they would both paint. Mostly, Prudence played on her own while her father worked. When Arthur and Prudence came home from the studio, Betty prepared an elaborate dinner, no matter how tired she was from work. Dinner was an important time of family togetherness. Afterwards, Betty would help Prudence with her homework. Though these arrangements were unconventional for their time, Betty did her best to be a "traditional" housewife and mother, and Prudence enjoyed closeness with both parents.

By the time he was 83, Arthur had long grown accustomed to Betty's constant support and companionship, and their lives had become even more entwined during their retirement years. Arthur was both realitybased and prone to denial – like many of us, a curiously mixed personality. It was difficult for him to see Betty as less than stalwart; nevertheless, he recognized that she had begun to decline. He wanted things to continue much the same, so he strove to compensate for her debilities. When it became clear that she was not able to manage her medications, he took over this function and did a remarkably efficient job of it. When she became confused about money, he did not have the heart to tell her that she could no longer carry any, but instead simply limited the amount in her purse. When she began to get lost in the neighborhood where they had resided for over 45 years, he made sure either he or a friend or neighbor accompanied her. Arthur's own good health, devotion to his wife, and creative management made it possible for Betty to remain at home.

Prudence lived only an hour and a half away from her parents, but she did not realize that Arthur was burdened with more than he could carry. Betty's illnesses had made Prudence well aware that her mother was frail and dependent, so Prudence stopped by every weekend to help out. In addition, she hired a cleaning service and paid a neighbor to take care of the shopping. However, Prudence also understood how important it was to Arthur that he care for Betty himself, and she was afraid of upsetting him. Thus, instead of listening to her better judgment, she allowed Arthur to convince her that he could manage things on his own during the week.

Finally, circumstances forced Arthur to speak realistically to Prudence about her mother's decline. One day, Betty slipped and fell as Arthur was helping her into the bathtub. Betty's injuries were not serious, but Arthur finally realized that Betty needed more assistance on a daily basis than he could provide. He warned Prudence that the time was coming when Betty might not be able to live at home, even under Arthur's watchful and loving eye. Because father and daughter could dialogue honestly and openly, they were able to assess the situation and to formulate reasonable and appropriate plans. Right away, they hired a full-time home health aide to bathe Betty and to tend to her physical and medical needs. Next, they researched and discussed their options for the longer term. Arthur insisted that every attempt should be made to keep husband and wife together. If Betty's condition forced a separation, Arthur must remain in close proximity to her. This one factor made planning considerably easier, since father and daughter knew a central variable as they contemplated possibilities.

Prudence suggested that her parents should come live with her. This would force them to leave the old neighborhood, but the benefits were obvious. Prudence could help watch over Betty, and she could cook her parents' meals, drive her mother to doctor's appointments, and take over the duties of the home health aide. Prudence had plans drawn up to modify her house, making the family room into a bedroom and adding a shower to the adjacent half-bathroom.

While all this was quite feasible, Arthur raised the issue of not becoming a burden on his daughter. Prudence assured him that this would not be the case and that she could even secure inexpensive supervision for her mother by hiring local college students. Nevertheless, Arthur continued to worry. He requested that they explore other possibilities.

One of the facilities they investigated was a senior apartment complex less than one mile from Prudence's home. This complex included a communal eating area, a dayroom, beautiful grounds, and transportation to malls and other recreational facilities. Maid service, home meals, additional supervision, and other support services were available when needed. An extended care facility was next door, so that husband and wife would be less than a block away if one of them needed to recuperate from an illness. Arthur thought that this complex would provide the perfect arrangement: he and Betty could stay together, and Prudence would be nearby, but not directly burdened with her parents' care. When Arthur put in an application, however, father and daughter were surprised to discover that there was a waiting list over a year long! Neither had even considered that such a complication could arise.

While Prudence was renovating her home and helping Arthur pack, Betty died. Arthur went ahead and moved in with Prudence, for Betty's absence pained him greatly. Being in a new environment, near his daughter, made Arthur's adjustment to life without his soul mate a little less difficult.

Though their final decision about Betty's future was never realized, Arthur and Prudence were greatly relieved to dialogue openly about Betty's condition, to investigate their options, and to make plans. Instead of wringing their hands and fretting about the possibilities, instead of concocting horror stories about what might happen, they confronted their fears and worries together, and together they took action.

Without Betty, Arthur and Prudence pursued plans of a different sort. They agreed that Arthur would stay with Prudence for as long as possible. Arthur made Prudence swear that she would have him admitted to an extended care facility as soon as he needed full-time assistance. Together, they researched appropriate facilities in the area, and Arthur chose two that suited him. Fortunately, Arthur's health is good, and it may be a while before he needs to move. However, when the time comes, Prudence will be able to make the arrangements that her father prefers.

Talk to your aged parents and begin to discuss your fears and concerns now. Plan together for the future. Mobilize your anxieties into mutual dialogue and collective action. Do not stagnate in isolated worry; be open with each other and draw upon your collective strengths. Plan for the eventualities rather than allowing yourself to be overwhelmed by them; doing so will make your present more bearable and your future more predictable.

Up to this point, our discussion has concerned positive mechanisms that led to meaningful outcomes. Sometimes, this is not what occurs, despite even the best efforts. Let us look at the story of an adult child who had a deep love and sense of responsibility for her aged parent, but cared for her in such a way that their situation became increasingly painful and difficult.

Magda was a 92-year-old woman who resided with her daughter Nadia in a suburban community on the outskirts of a major metropolitan area. Magda was born in the Midwest in 1902. Her father was a tradesman while her mother cared for the children. These people were poor, and life was quite difficult for them. Magda's father worked from daylight well into the night, trying to earn enough money to feed the family. After the domestic chores were done, Magda's mother would help out in whatever way she could to earn additional funds.

Magda was a bright child and did exceptionally well in school. She read voraciously, spending many afternoons and evenings in the public library. At age 15, however, she had to quit school and get a full-time job to help supplement the family income. She enrolled in night school, and eventually received her diploma. These years were so filled with work and school that there was little time to play. Despite hardship and deprivation, Magda and her family persevered.

At age 19, Magda began to work as a secretary in a law firm. Her intelligence and ability to learn quickly were soon recognized, and she went through a series of promotions. Also at this time, she met and married a promising young man who was making his way in the local business community. Over the next few years, Magda's husband prospered, so Magda was able to quit her job and become a full-time homemaker. She did not forget her parents in her new affluence, and proved to be an attentive and generous daughter.

Soon Magda and her husband had a daughter. Nadia was a lucky child, for she not only had parents who loved her, but she also enjoyed material advantages such as her mother had never known. For example, Nadia had her own room in a spacious house and plenty of food, toys, and clothes – amenities many of us take for granted, but which were luxuries for Magda.

Still, despite Magda's prosperity, vestiges of her own deprived childhood remained with her and affected her relationship with Nadia. For example, Magda was preoccupied with food. She did not feel comfortable unless there was an abundance on hand, and she insisted that whatever was prepared had to be eaten in its entirety. According to Nadia, Madga stocked the kitchen with enough food to feed ten people. In addition, she always prepared huge meals, and everything she heaped on Nadia's plate had to be consumed, down to the last crumb – there was no such thing as leftovers in this house.

Magda's preoccupation was the direct result of her childhood experience. She had grown up in poverty, and she needed to reassure herself that she and her family would never face deprivation again. As a child, Magda had worried whether there would be food on the table each day. Now, there was plenty, but she still felt desperate to make sure that Nadia would never go hungry the way she had. Having an abundance around at all times not only guaranteed survival, but also relieved Magda's anxiety and fear. Because food was so precious, wasting it was a terrible sin.

Magda pushed food on Nadia in a desperate attempt to nurture her and keep her safe. This act of love was perceived quite differently by Nadia, however. Nadia had never known deprivation, so she experienced her mother's behavior as domineering and oppressive. She came to loathe dinner time. There was no way of avoiding what she thought of as her mother's craziness. If Nadia refused food, Magda became upset and even more adamant. At age 14, Nadia developed a set of symptoms that enabled her both to appease her mother and to fend off her own anxiety and stress. Nadia became bulimic.

Thus, food became an issue of control for both mother and daughter. As a child, Magda had feared for her very survival; as an adult, she made sure that her family would never go hungry by constantly over-feeding them. Nadia felt forced to eat more than she wanted by an anxious and imperious mother; purging herself after dinner became a way to avoid conflict and still assert control over her own body. The solution to Magda's problems was the cause of Nadia's, yet both mother and daughter were trying to cope with significant trauma resulting from the unstable envi-ronments in which they lived.

Nadia found another way to adapt to the situation: she would often feign illnesses in order to be excused from meals and thus from the negative interface with her mother they always brought. This strategy produced an added benefit: when Nadia was on her sickbed, Magda was sensitive and solicitous.

Another dysfunctional interface between mother and daughter involved dependency needs. Magda always felt safe at home; however, she feared the uncontrollable world outside. When Nadia ventured out into the world as she grew older – a normal developmental pattern – she fre-quently felt undermined by her mother's anxiety. For example, when Nadia went to school dances, Magda worried that some disaster might befall her while she was out of her mother's protective reach. Magda's fears about Nadia's ability to take care of herself caused Nadia to approach her blossoming independence with ambivalence, for Nadia could not help but adopt some of her mother's feelings. As a result, she had difficulty letting go of her mother's apron strings, even when she felt the urge to strike out on her own most strongly.

Eventually, all these difficulties led Nadia and Magda into therapy. They saw a psychiatrist for quite some time. Unfortunately, treatment did not resolve their conflicts. It did, however, help them reach a mutual accommodation. Nadia learned to confront her mother directly rather than symptomatically, and stopped her bulimic behavior and feigned ill-nesses, while Magda learned to listen to her daughter and to separate her needs from Nadia's. Respect for each other's point of view allowed the relationship between these women to progress more calmly and with considerably less stress. Furthermore, Magda and Nadia developed a deeper love for one another. After Nadia left home, she and her mother became good friends, often lunching and vacationing together. Nadia had developed many of her mother's positive traits, not the least of which was a desire to nurture.

After Nadia married, Magda remained an integral part of her daughter's life. Although there was now some geographical distance between them, they often made the trip in order to spend a day together. They met regularly on holidays and continued to vacation together.

After Nadia's father died, Magda started her own business dealing in art and antiques. She filled her home with paintings and other art objects, and she invited customers over for brunch, serving them – characteristically – an abundance of fine food. Meanwhile, Nadia also gravitated toward the arts and eventually opened her own jewelry design and sales shop. She used some of her mother's techniques to develop relationships with her customers. Both women were successful.

As the years passed, Nadia became only minimally aware of Magda's aging. She clung to the image of her mother as a strong and resourceful woman who had risen above difficult circumstances and become successful in both family and business. Nadia also maintained her childhood impression of Magda as domineering. Thus, she did not notice when Magda began to forget the details of her dealings with customers. In Nadia's mind, Magda remained the powerful and competent person she had always been. Over time, however, Magda's physical stamina and mental acuity deteriorated significantly. She became undeniably less functional, and the signs of her decline began to show more obtrusively.

As Magda became more aware of her own decline, she also became more anxious. Her distress did not take the form of fear of aging, but rather manifested as a need to restrict her environment. She felt in control at home, but increasingly out of control whenever she stepped forth into the world. Occasionally, she might venture the familiar territory of her immediate neighborhood or her daughter's house, but now she never ventured the unexplored. Magda was attempting to compensate for her deficiencies. Like many elderly people, she stuck to the familiar, thereby minimizing the chances that she would feel lost. Whenever her deficiences made an appearance at home, she could contain and work around them. For example, on occasions when customers caught her unprepared because she had forgotten they were coming, she could easily recover her composure by taking comfort in the familiarity of her surroundings. She did not dare to risk such mistakes in unfamiliar and potentially threatening environments.

Gradually, Magda had greater and greater difficulty in functioning on her own. Because Nadia did not pick up the clues, however, she did not see the necessity of planning for her mother's needs. Intellectually, Nadia knew that the day would come when her mother would require assistance. She was unable to recognize her mother's current condition because – like so many of us – she was not ready to accept it on an *emotional* level. Instead, she deluded herself and ignored the warning signs. We could fault her for not seeing reality, but fault is not the issue here. It takes courage as well as awareness to see our aging parents as they really are, for we must give up our image of them as powerful nurturers, and accept the idea that they are becoming frail and dependent. Instead of faulting Nadia, we should learn from her mistakes.

Magda colluded with Nadia by fostering the illusion that nothing had changed. Magda hid her failures and periods of confusion from her daughter, and presented herself as the competent mother she had always been. This is not uncommon behavior. Often, aged parents do not want to allow their once-dependent children to become their caretakers. It is hard enough for our parents to admit to the subtler ravages of the aging process; but it is even harder for them to give up the image of themselves as responsible adults who not only function independently, but also take care of others. This is the self-image they have harbored throughout the majority of their lives. They internalized it as young children when they admired how their own parents nurtured them; they lived by it as they nurtured us; they persisted in it even after we grew to adulthood and developed our own lives. Now, they are faced with the terrible and difficult realization that they are no longer the people they thought they were and – moreover – that their condition can only worsen. For many aged parents, the defensive posture of denial and selective perception becomes automatic: they cover up the evidence to avoid the inevitable conclusion and the pain that it brings.

This is what Magda did. She found ways to hide her deficiencies, from herself as well as others. Meanwhile, Nadia was ensconced in her own delusions. Because these two did not deal with the changes in Magda's life in an open and ongoing dialogue, they were overtaken by a reality that they had failed to foresee. As a result, they entered a new phase of their relationship: the unprepared adult child became the caretaker of her aged mother, and the proud and reluctant mother became increasingly dependent upon her unprepared and eventually overburdened adult child.

Magda's mental decline suddenly accelerated. She forgot the day of the week; she forgot appointments; she became confused when people called her on the phone. Of course, as these lapses happened, she still sought to explain them away. She was and always had been very personable, and she could call upon her charm to make things seem less drastic than they actually were. It was quite natural for her to compensate for her mistakes with an amusing apology, and she was so well liked in her circle that it took only a few words to divert people from noticing her decline. Also, Magda's lifestyle lent itself to such deceptions. While she had many friends and business associates, she rarely spent an extended time with any of them, and the cheery glimpses of her they obtained, along with her charming and amusing explanations, masked her increasing dysfunction for a long time.

Nadia did see signs of change in Magda, since she phoned her often and saw her regularly. What she did not see, however, was how far Magda had declined. When they spoke on the phone, Nadia could tell that her mother was not as sharp as she had been. Since their conversations were brief, however, the extent of Magda's confusion was not readily evident. When Nadia visited, Magda made a great effort to appear normal. She usually arranged for other people to join them, so she could manage the situation and camouflage her difficulty. Nadia missed the significance of Magda's actions. She regarded the presence of others as a sign that Magda still had a full and active social life.

Magda avoided spending extended periods of time with anyone. She did not wish to see herself in a way that was degrading and embarrassing, nor did she want to burden friends and family with her difficulties. She believed that if she could continue to adapt to the changes in her life, she would be fine. When the extent of her dysfunction grew beyond her ability to compensate, however, she was no longer adapting to but rather *masking* her difficulties. Instead of directing her skills and energy toward achieving a reasonable quality of life, she was using them to maintain the illusion that life could progress as it had before.

Nadia unknowingly colluded in this fantasy. By visiting not quite so often, by choosing to blend into the social scene at her mother's house, and by accepting her mother's explanations and apologies, Nadia could easily ignore the reality of the situation. This was not done out of malice or insensitivity, but rather out of a deep desire to hold on to life as it was when it was good.

This is a well-known psychological mechanism. When life becomes hard, the memories of times when life was better linger in our consciousness, though most of us find it possible to differentiate between present reality and past triumph. For example, someone who once lived in a luxurious mansion may close his eyes on his studio apartment and remember the good times, but he still recognizes the difference between now and then. Indeed, recalling the image of what he had before could spur him to make back his fortune. But what if he had to reconcile himself to the fact that no matter what he did, no matter how hard he tried, he could never regain his former lifestyle? And not only that, but his studio apartment would grow smaller and smaller until it became a cell, and then he must depend on other people to care for his most basic needs? *It is a thousand times more difficult to accept a decline that is irreversible.* And what if you had to watch someone you loved undergo such a decline, and you could do nothing to stop it? No wonder we cling to our illusions!

This analogy brings home what all of us must face in dealing with our aged parents. We will have to watch them slip and drift into increasing dysfunction, helpless to stop the process. The best we can do is ensure that they maintain a reasonable quality of life as they age. We can walk alongside them through this stage of life; we can be there so that they are not alone; we can comfort them when they are afraid, talk to them when they are lonely, and let them know that we love them and that we will never abandon them. Before we can do any of this, however, we must face the reality of their decline.

In facing that reality, we cannot escape another − that if we become our parents' parents, in effect, we are orphaned. We must give up the security of being children; we must give up the idea that we will always have someone to run to when we are in trouble or to protect us when we are afraid. This is a very difficult leap to make, for it is sad as well as daunting.

We must meet the challenge of this transition openly and honestly and with courage, sensitivity, and understanding. There is an inevitable role reversal in the cycle of life: we become the caretakers of those who once took care of us. Parents and children who can acknowledge this fact and do whatever it takes to adjust to it will have a good chance of proceeding through the transition with minimal difficulty and trauma. Parents and children who deny or evade reality will drift into or be overwhelmed by circumstances that will only increase their pain. Of course, life rarely offers black and white situations, and discrepant perceptions are more likely to be the rule. The adult child may accept reality, but his aged parent may deny it and resist all efforts to help. Or the aged parent may view his decline stoically and pragmatically, but the adult child refuses to acknowledge it, leaving the parent feeling isolated and abandoned as well as in need of assistance. Whatever the circumstances, adjusting to reality is the goal, and open communication is the best way to reach it.

Unfortunately, both Magda and Nadia denied the reality they faced, and each fostered the other's illusion that life could proceed as it always had. That is, until circumstances forced reality upon them.

It happened suddenly. Magda was home alone, trying to hang a painting, when she lost her balance and fell off the stepladder. She was hurt, and almost a whole day passed before anyone came to her aid. Of course, she should not have been on the ladder in the first place; but Nadia had not yet figured out that Magda needed someone else to perform such tasks. As a result, Magda lay on the floor for many hours in pain, unable to stand, without food or water, defecating and urinating in her clothes, conscious but unable to do anything about her condition. At last, a customer rang her bell. When no one answered, she told a neighbor, who called Nadia.

Magda was hospitalized and recovered quickly. After a few days, she was ready to be discharged. Her injuries were not serious, but the incident forced Nadia finally to recognize that her mother could no longer live on her own. She began to make plans for Magda to give up the house. When she broached the subject with her mother, however, Magda became indignant. Despite the accident, Magda was still in denial. At first, she refused to consider the idea; she was hurt and upset that Nadia had such a low opinion of her. Both women expressed anger and frustration and both cried as they discussed the situation over the next several days. Before the accident, they had made a habit of suppressing their feelings; now, in the wake of a traumatic event, they had to deal with all of them in a concentrated form.

Magda experienced rage at her decline and intense frustration over her lack of choices and over the possibility of losing her independence. Nadia felt guilty for not having recognized her mother's needs sooner, but she also felt guilty for making her mother so upset. In addition, she felt daunted by her new position as caretaker, and saddened by the fact that she would no longer be under her mother's protection. Each woman had to manage her intense feelings interactively. That is, each had to express herself to the other and respond to the other's feelings in an attempt to reach an accommodation, so that together they could plan for the future. Because mother and daughter were at different stages in their recognition of reality, these interactions were very painful.

Magda and Nadia eventually agreed that Magda would come to Nadia's home to recuperate for a few weeks. As the weeks passed, Magda settled in gradually. She began to realize that life was much easier when she had her daughter's help. She no longer felt the pressure of having to hide her dysfunctional behavior. She was pleased to contribute by helping with meals. After about three months, she agreed to stay at her daughter's permanently, and arrangements were made to sell her own house and move all her possessions to Nadia's.

Nadia had not planned to have her mother move into her home on a permanent basis. In fact, she had never really considered the possibility. When Magda was in the hospital, Nadia had inquired about elder care facilities and nursing homes. Because she had not planned ahead, she was surprised to learn that there were long waiting lists for the better facilities in her area. Nadia put her mother on a few of these lists; while they waited for an opening, however, Magda became so comfortable at Nadia's house that the idea of having to make another change, this time to an unfamiliar environment, set off a great deal of anxiety and resistance in her.

If Nadia and her mother had planned for such a transition in an open dialogue, it could have been accomplished with much less difficulty. However, there had been little discussion and no planning, so Magda made a transition from independence in her own home to dependence in her daughter's, and, once she settled in, it became increasingly difficult to get her to consider other options. Nadia thought about forcing Magda to move, but she feared that such a maneuver would only accelerate her mother's decline. Nadia loved her mother very deeply, and she did not want to hurt her. To avoid making matters worse, she allowed Magda to remain in her home permanently. Nadia obtained support services as they were needed, but inevitably Magda became a tremendous burden on her. Living up to her commitment took a great toll upon Nadia, compromising her freedom and lifestyle, and leading to considerable expense. Life progressed in this manner until Magda died in her bed in Nadia's home. While Nadia missed her mother, her mother's care had become such a burden to her that she felt relief as well as grief.

There is an important lesson to be learned from the story of Magda and Nadia. *We must strive to be aware of the changes in our aged parents as they decline.* These changes are psychological as well as physical and mental – and they are inevitable. Ignoring them now will only increase the pain and suffering when we deal with them later. We must broach the subject *now;* we must engage in an *ongoing* dialogue with our parents that is sensitive as well as candid. All of us, both parents and children, must deal with our emotions and grieve for our lost illusions. We must face reality together if we are to plan for the future and find solutions that will work for everyone.

Let us make this painful phase of life not only tolerable, but meaningful; let us grow together with our aged parents rather than apart from them; let us benefit even in the midst of decline and painful change!

I can remember when the idea of my mother's mortality first occurred to me. I got an emergency call to come to New York right away. My mother, at age 62, had suffered a heart attack, and it looked as if she might not make it. I was even told to come directly from the airport to the hospital for fear of arriving too late to see her. On the plane, I was occupied by memories of my mother, and I cried intermittently. I recalled how she had always been nurturing and loving. I wished that I could somehow fix what was wrong with her. I would have done anything or given anything to make her well. I was dumbfounded. How could my mother be dying before I was ready to be without her? It was, of course, foolish of me not to have seen the warning signs that I had noticed in others so astutely: she smoked heavily and had for years; she was overweight; she never exercised. By all rights, I should have considered the eventuality of a heart attack. In fact, I should have expected it, given her lifestyle. But the thought had never even crossed my mind! Thus, it was with a sense of disbelief that I found myself on a plane speeding to my mother's bedside, not knowing if she would be alive or dead when I arrived, hoping and praying that I would find her alive and in good spirits.

My mother's illness had caught me unprepared. I had spoken to her only a few days before and assumed that all was well. I had lived in the illusion to which so many of us unwittingly subscribe: I had fully accepted as reality the idea that tomorrow will be much the same as today, that life flows predictably and nothing terrible will ever happen. How much we trust to the mechanism of denial! Terrible things do happen and can occur without warning at any time. Something terrible was happening to my mother and thus to me, and I was both shocked and frightened. It took a lot of effort to push down my fears and focus on my mother's plight.

This time she survived and recovered, and we were blessed to have her for another 18 years, though in an ever-declining state that was sharply punctuated with medical crises. It took me some weeks to process this experience and to give up the fantasy that life is predictable. I was forced to think of my mother differently. I became acutely aware of her frailty, and I realized that our roles had changed. No longer was she the mother who always took care of me and always would. I had to come to grips with the fact that it was now my turn to look after her. I must tend to her needs and plan for her future.

I was not alone in this realization. My brothers and my father were facing the same painful reality. Now, we must together consider the inevitability of her death and strive to make the quality of her life the best possible.

Of course, this realization also led me to the idea of my own mortality. My mother's illness forced me to acknowledge that she would die at some point, as would my father, and that I would be the next in line. A simple logical thought, but how difficult on an emotional level! I still struggle with it at times.

Over the next 18 years, we faced a number of frightening events when my mother's life was in grave danger. My mother developed breast cancer and underwent a mastectomy. Then, she had a heart defibrillation. Next, it was bypass surgery. In between, we watched her deteriorate with Alzheimer's. Each crisis reminded us that her life was fragile and her death was imminent. My father, my brothers, and I endeavored to maintain a good quality of life for her and to anticipate her needs and look out for her interests. In retrospect, it seems odd that it was these tragic events that kept us united and focused on our goal.

Eventually, my mother died. We had to deal with losing her, but at least we did so with the knowledge that we had recognized and responded to her needs. We did not have to regret missed opportunities. Though our grief was great, we took comfort in knowing that we had acted on her behalf.

CHAPTER FOUR

THE PROBLEMS WE FACE
IN HELPING THEM

As we have seen in the previous chapters, the aging process brings on increasing debility and dependence. If we are to be of any help to our aged parents as they experience this process, we must make a realistic, ongoing assessment of their changing needs. We must be aware of each phase of their decline *as it happens,* so we can take steps to help them to adapt to it and to prepare for the next phase. In the course of these changes, we adult children also experience a painful process. As we shoulder more and more responsibility as caregivers, we gradually lose the strength and support of our parents. In this sense, there are two "saying good-byes" to mom and dad. The good-bye that we say to them when they die is anticipated by the good-bye that we say as we watch them relinquish their role as parents and become increasingly dependent upon us for support and nurturance.

Saying the first good-bye is not easy. It is difficult to let go of the pattern of family life that formerly existed. Before, our parents took care of us and never really needed our care. Now, not only must we be fully responsible for ourselves; we must also be responsible for the physical and emotional well-being of our aged parents. This change in our role requires a difficult psychological shift. We must face a great loss and a daunting set of responsibilities. Compounding this difficulty is the inescapable conclusion that our role will change yet again. Life is cyclical; like our parents, we too will one day become increasingly dependent and in need of care. We too will age and die. Thus, saying the first good-bye to our aged parents forces us to explore new emotional territory.

Our aging parents are also exploring new emotional territory. After all, if it is hard for us to say good-bye to the strong people they once were, imagine how hard it must be for them to say good-bye to their younger selves, and to accept being taken care of by the very children they once nurtured and protected! Even if our parents are unafraid of death – and many are afraid – they still must grapple with the pain and humiliation of decline and dependency. We must be sensitive to the emotional challenges they are facing if we are to act effectively, compassionately, and meaningfully. We must open a dialogue with our aged parents now, when we have the time to come to terms with these changes, to anticipate those ahead of us and to adjust to those that have already occurred.

Aging is a process we go through all of our lives, a normal progression that involves a variety of biological, psychological, and social changes over time. The quality of our lives as we grow older can vary greatly according to genetic predispositions, lifestyle choices, and environmental factors.

All people are born with certain biological and genetic potentialities. Many of these are positive, but others are potentially destructive, such as predispositions to diabetes or high cholesterol. In general, these biological realities will emerge in time, though in some instances it may be within our power to minimize their effects. For example, a person predisposed to high cholesterol can exercise and restrict his diet to forestall the condition, or take medication to control symptoms should they occur. Indeed, our biological destinies are affected greatly by lifestyle choices. The choice to smoke, for example, increases the probability of lung cancer, hypertension, and other circulatory difficulties. The choice to eat a diet high in animal fats increases the probability of cardiovascular disease. The choice not to exercise leaves the body less able to function optimally, so that muscles are not as strong as they could be, joints lose range of motion, and the circulatory system grows less competent.

Lifestyle and genetics also interact with environmental factors. A patient of mine reported that she grew up near a large chemical plant. She and her six siblings used to play in a drainage ditch that ran near their house. The drainage was largely uncontrolled waste from the plant, and years later she and all six of her siblings developed various types of cancer.

In addition to these factors, the aging process also involves a psychological dimension. *Attitude,* for example, plays a major part. How we feel about aging and about being old affects how we age and how we act toward others as they age. Someone who is afraid to grow old is less likely to recognize his aged parent's need for assistance; this is because recognizing the need requires a shift in perspective that implicates him in the aging process. An aged parent's attitude toward being old can lead to a variety of responses. Commonly, older parents are reluctant to admit that they need help. As a point of pride, they may resist giving up their autonomy; or they may be wary of becoming a burden on us. We adult children must take care not to comply with their resistance. If we are to ensure the highest quality of life for our parents, we must strive to see their condition realistically. Denying reality and fostering illusions will do nothing to improve our parents' current situation, and can only lead to more painful consequences down the road.

Let us look at the story of a woman who had great difficulty accepting the aging process and whose behavior inhibited her adult children from being as helpful to her as they could have been.

Diane is a 74-year-old widow. She lives alone in an older adult apartment complex. She requires little assistance and manages on her own quite adequately. She was married for 43 years, but her husband died of pancreatic cancer about ten years earlier. Diane's husband was a druggist by trade. For a number of years, he had his own store and the family lived quite well. When the discount chains came into the neighborhood, however, he could not compete with their prices and was forced to liquidate his business and work for such a chain. This led to a significant drop in income, and the lifestyle of the family declined. After her husband's death, Diane had to live on a modest fixed income. She moved into an old age complex where a number of her friends, also widowed, resided. Diane was only gainfully employed from age 16 until she was married at age 21. She had no marketable skills and little education. Her children, however, have done quite well. Her daughter, Ellen, 49, has a master's degree in education and is a special education coordinator. She is divorced with two grown children. Diane's son Paul, 51, is a college professor who never married.

When Diane was 40, her mother died a slow and difficult death from cancer. This had a profound impact on Diane, and she developed an intense fear of illness as a result. She worried constantly about contracting some form of disease. When she watched medical dramas on television, she worried that she felt some of the characters' symptoms. Whenever a friend had a physical complaint, Diane worried that she might get the same thing. She bought every over-the-counter product she saw advertised, until she heard about a woman who died because she had taken a combination of the same medicines. Diane's anxieties about her health affected her children's upbringing. For example, Paul and Ellen grew up having to wear scarves when they went out so as not to "catch cold," as

Diane put it, and for a while they had to endure enemas for the purpose of cleansing their systems.

Two themes emerged from the trauma of Diane's experience of her mother's protracted and painful disease. There was the fear of becoming ill, as we have seen. In addition, there was the fear of becoming dependent upon others. Diane had seen her mother gradually lose her ability to function independently. She knew what a burden her mother's care had become on those around her, so she vowed never to let that happen to herself. She protected herself in two ways. First, she was vigilant about the health of her loved ones, so that she would not have to revisit the trauma of her mother's illness. Second, she was intensely vigilant about her own health, so that she would never be a burden on anyone else.

As Diane grew older, her fear of dependence played out for her children in difficult ways. Whenever Paul or Ellen wanted to do something for their mother, Diane resisted. One time, Ellen realized that her mother's coat was worn, so she took it upon herself to purchase a new coat in a style her mother favored. When she gave Diane the coat, however, instead of being appreciative, Diane became angry. She felt insulted that Ellen did not believe her capable of buying her own coat, and insisted that the coat be returned. Ellen did not visit her mother for a long time afterwards. She was deeply offended by the incident, for she took the rejection of the coat as a rejection of herself. Ellen had recognized her mother's need, but she had not looked for a way to accommodate her mother's idiosyncrasies. As a result, Ellen was ineffective in caring for the aged parent who needed her.

This is a trap many adult children fall into. Instead of understanding the issues that motivate parental behavior, they become embroiled in the actions themselves; as a result, they grow resentful and become unavailable to help. Paul had a similar experience when he offered to buy his mother a condominium in Florida. He wanted her to get away from the harsh winters she faced where she lived. Diane, of course, would not agree to this. After all, what would happen if Paul lost his job and could not make the payments? This response frustrated Paul. As he saw it, his mother had rejected his gift; she simply would not allow him to help her. Like Ellen, he was hurt, so he withdrew. The upshot, however, was that Diane remained in her cold apartment.

Thus, Diane's attitude about becoming dependent was inhibiting her loving adult children from improving the quality of her life as she grew older. Ellen and Paul felt shut out. Whenever they confronted their mother, Diane would somehow turn the topic to health-related issues. She might say, "How can you upset a poor old woman who could get sick at any time?" This usually stopped Paul and Ellen from pursuing the issue, not because they believed it, but because they knew that Diane would not hear any more input from them once she started talking about illness.

Not knowing what to do, Paul and Ellen discussed the situation with a physician friend who referred them to me. During the consultation, I helped them to understand the dynamic that was underlying Diane's entrenched behavior, to comprehend how Diane's traumatic experience with her mother had distorted her perspective. Because she had witnessed her mother's slow decline into ever-increasing dependence, Diane knew and was terrified of both sides of the equation: on the one side, she did not want to burden her children with the pain she had gone through; on the other, she did not want to reexperience the trauma by having to care for a sick family member. With this understanding, Paul and Ellen could free themselves of their personal hurt and begin to see both why their mother rejected their help and why she was so preoccupied with health.

We worked out a basic strategy for Paul and Ellen that proved effective in dealing with their mother. They must indirectly allay Diane's fears so that she could accept their help. For example, when Ellen again wanted to give her mother a coat, this time she said, "Mom, I know you have a perfectly good coat, but there was a sale, and I got this coat at an unbelievable price. I bought it for myself, but it's too small. Maybe it will fit you. I can't return it, and I'd rather give it to you than to some stranger." Ellen began by reassuring Diane of her autonomy; then she framed the offer in such a way that her mother could accept it, even if reluctantly, without feeling dependent. The gift was the same, but this time it was wrapped differently! Using a similar strategy, Paul was able to move Diane to Florida for the winter. He bought a condominium for himself as an investment and rented it out part of the year. From November to March, he rented it to his mother. He charged her a minimal amount of rent and showed her how, from a business standpoint, she was actually helping him to make money. Being a tenant instead of a charity case made Diane feel useful instead of burdensome. Paul achieved his goal of keeping Diane warm for the winter by presenting an arrangement that appealed to her way of looking at things and thus reduced her anxieties. Some might view the children's strategies as manipulative, but they were merely a means of acting on Diane's behalf while taking into account her idiosyncratic perspective. Because Paul and Ellen understood their mother's thinking, they were able to communicate with her when the issue of dependence was present. As a result, they were able to bypass her resistance and improve the quality of her life. Of course, not all of us will encounter such a difficult situation. Nevertheless, if we take care to recognize who our parents are now and how they look at the world, a more collaborative approach to the problems that arise in their lives is possible.

The difficulties in the story just examined centered around the aged parent's attitude about dependency issues. In other cases, the problem revolves around the related theme of control. As our parents age, the symptoms of physical or cognitive decline make them feel increasingly out of control. Many parents try to compensate for this feeling by controlling whatever they can. For example, they may manipulate the adult children so they are always at their beck and call. In such cases, while it appears that the aged parents are domineering and excessively demanding, the underlying basis for their behavior is usually a fear of being abandoned, of being left alone without help when they need it. Insecurity, then, is the prime motivation in such behavior. As our parents see themselves becoming less and less functional, and as they see their friends and neighbors falling ill, having tragic mishaps, and dying, they begin to worry about their own future. They may fail to recognize how many of their contemporaries are actually doing well.

It is important for us to recognize that our aged parents are affected not only by what is happening to them, but also by what is happening in their environment and by how they interpret or evaluate these events. I remember an elderly woman who became run down. It took some probing to find out why. For years, she had always bought her meat from a butcher she trusted. He only carried the finest quality, and he always chatted and joked with her when she came into the shop. Eventually, however, this butcher retired and moved away, and the woman had to buy her meat from the local supermarket. This place, however, was large and impersonal. She began to criticize the supermarket, claiming that the meat was not of the same quality as her old butcher's. Finally, she stopped buying meat altogether. This response, of course, had nothing to do with the quality of the meat. In fact, the woman was reacting to the loss of a friend, of a cherished routine, of a personal service that was very important to her. The point here is that elderly people encounter a great deal of change in their lives for which they are not prepared. Any change in their behavior may signal a reaction to some change in their environment. It behooves us to listen to them and to inquire about what is happening in their lives, so that we can be more aware of what they are really dealing with, and then take steps to help them.

It is crucial that we listen to our aging parents. Listening informs us about their lives and allows them to express their feelings. We need to give our aged parents many opportunities to speak. Sometimes, they will talk about superficial things, but even superficial conversation can be revealing. For example, the woman's complaints about the meat at the supermarket, which might have seemed insignificant to a casual listener, were in fact linked to important issues – her feelings of loss and her weakening health. It is not enough, then, just to listen or to let our parents talk. *We must be good listeners.* We must read between the lines and interpret what they are saying. If our parents tell us about an elderly person next door who had a heart attack, we must consider the possibility that our parents are afraid that this could happen to them, or that they are sad and lonely now that their friend is gone, or that they feel abandoned or insecure. In the course of the conversation, we must explore these themes to see if they are in fact present. We will not understand, however, unless we have first listened sensitively and considered what our aged parents have described in relation to their current situation. That is to say, we must put ourselves in their shoes, we must view the world from their perspective, if we are to understand fully the changes that are occurring in their lives. We must listen keenly, interpret carefully, and check out our conclusions thoroughly. Only in this way can we respond empathically, realistically, and tactfully to the dilemmas they face.

Let us see how all of these factors interact in the lives of real people.

Mike had a difficult time dealing with his 79-year-old mother, Fran. Fran seemed to be demanding more and more of his time. She called him several times a day to talk, frequently about what Mike thought were minor occurrences. She never ended a conversation without asking Mike to call her soon. She wanted him to stop by to see her at least once a day. If he missed a day or two, she would become angry and sulk and pout, and Mike would feel guilty. But Mike had a life of his own. He worked as a mid-level supervisor for the Secretary of State's office in his city. He had his own family and, although his children were grown, he liked to visit them and his grandchildren as much as he could. He and his wife belonged to a mixed doubles bowling league, and he had a hobby of restoring old automobiles. Mike, then, was quite frustrated with his mother's constant demands. If he visited her as often as she required, he lost time for his other activities; if he skipped a visit, he had to contend with her childlike tantrums.

Fran lived a few miles away from her son, in an apartment she had taken after her husband had passed away ten years before. When her husband was alive, most of Fran's dependency needs were met by him. After his death, however, Fran came to rely more and more on Mike. Fran's health was not good. She was ambulatory, but she had emphysema and needed oxygen periodically. She rarely ventured out of her apartment except for doctor's appointments. When family events occurred, she insisted either that they take place at her home or that Mike stop by afterwards to tell her about them. Fran had a lot of friends who came by to play cards or called her during the day, but she never went to their homes. All of these friends were elderly widows. At first, Mike thought they were in better health than Fran, but he later found out that one had cancer and another had bad arthritis that limited her mobility. The difference was that these other women had positive attitudes about life; they would not let pain and discomfort keep them from having meaningful experiences. Mike told me that the woman with cancer was fond of saying, "I may have one foot in the grave, but the other is still kicking." Mike marveled at these women's attitudes. He often wondered why his mother did not have a similarly positive attitude. It also surprised him how loyal these women were to his mother; apparently, Fran could be quite charming and empathic with her friends, but not with her son.

Fran was an only child who was born after her parents had experienced a number of miscarriages and had lost an infant to polio. She was her parents' miracle. They indulged and doted on her, giving her literally everything she wanted. One event characterizes the whole of Fran's upbringing. When Fran was eight, she became enthralled with the story of Black Beauty, and she wanted a horse of her own. Her parents pointed out that their urban lifestyle precluded having a horse, but Fran continued to voice her desire. Instead of simply stating that a horse was out of the question and ending the matter, her parents strove to please their little Fran, arranging for her to take riding lessons at a stable a considerable distance away and then buying her an expensive hobbyhorse that would move if she pushed down on the pedals.

Fran was a good student, but she frequently did things to be the center of attention. Unlike many women of her generation, Fran attended college for a year and a half until she married. Mike reports that his father was an extremely tolerant individual who doted on his wife, perhaps because he was 18 years older.

Mike remembers Fran as being an "OK" mother. She did the things she had to do. As he grew to adolescence, however, his mother relied more and more on him. She taught him to do the laundry because "he was not going to be a helpless man around the house," and soon he was doing laundry for the whole family. Ironing was also handled in this way, as were washing the dishes and vacuuming. In short, Mike remembers feeling like Cinderella: he had to do chores that none of his friends did while his mother did less and less.

As the years passed, Mike came to see his mother as a self-indulgent, self-centered person. When his father died, Mike was left with the job of caring for his mother, and he found himself back where he had been as an adolescent. Mike came to me for consultation because of his intense feelings of resentment towards his mother; he felt he had been exploited by her throughout most of his life, and he was angry about it. At the same time, his upbringing had left him with deep feelings of responsibility toward her. Furthermore, he felt he could not confront or cut off a 79-year-old woman in ill health. Here was quite a dilemma.

While I won't go into the complexity of Mike's treatment, which was arduous and successful, I will detail some practical strategies Mike used to solve the problem of Fran's demands.

Mike came to the conclusion that his mother needed to be in an elder care setting. In such a setting, she would be with other people the same age, and her friends could still visit. Above all, there would be 24-hour coverage for all her needs. Mike would be free to visit frequently, but he would not be responsible for his mother's care.

The problem was how to get Fran to accept this idea. Fran realized that her days of living in her own apartment were coming to a close. She had a sense of reality about her growing incapacities; after all, complaining about them had often brought her son to her side. Naturally, her proposed solution was to move in with Mike! When Mike figured out her plan, he became frantic. It was bad enough having to deal with his demanding mother from a distance; he could not fathom having her under his roof.

Mike's solution was quite effective. With the aid and support of his wife, he put his foot down gently. He made it clear to his mother that moving into his home was not an option. He stated that he loved her, but he did not want his life disrupted or his privacy with his wife destroyed. He made it clear that he and his wife had raised their family and had settled down to their own lifestyle, and they simply would not have this change. In addition, he made it clear that Fran's medical needs were progressive and that he was not able to meet them. Fran pouted and sulked and became angry. She did not speak to Mike for several days. But Mike was able to maintain his position; he had finally set a boundary, a limit to what he would and would not do. If he had done this sooner, he might have avoided those stressful years of feeling trapped and at his mother's beck and call. This time, however, he had drawn the line, and he would not allow his mother to cross it. Of course, this was not an easy thing for Mike to do. He had to deal with his own ambivalent feelings of anger and love. Furthermore, he had to acknowledge and work with his guilt. After all, how could a grown adult son turn his back on his sickly mother? This was the sort of question that his mother had used to manipulate him over the years, so it was natural for him to ask it of himself now. This time, however, there was a difference. He was able to recognize that, in reality, he was not turning his back. Rather, his solution was the most productive for everyone involved, since Fran needed more care than he could provide, and his own happiness with his wife counted.

Eventually, Fran softened her resistance. She agreed to visit some care facilities. One in particular appealed to her. It was near where Mike lived, and one of her friends was moving there. Mike helped moderate the impact of Fran's transition in several ways. When Fran had to decide what furniture to sell, Mike and his wife agreed to store anything she wanted to keep, but could not take to the elder care home. In addition, Mike made sure that Fran visited the home on a regular basis before the move, so she could sample the meals, attend some of the activities held there, and talk to the residents. Thus, when it came time to move, Fran was familiar with the routines of the place and with her new neighbors. Mike continued to help Fran adjust even after the move, stopping by daily and having Fran to dinner twice a week. Later on, after Fran had settled into her new surroundings, Mike was able to cut back on the amount of time he spent with her.

Thus, a difficult situation was dealt with effectively. Before he faced his issues, Mike had been only an adequate caregiver to Fran because he resented her demands. Fran, meanwhile, had experienced anxiety over receiving insufficient care. This fear had led her to become even more demanding, and she had driven Mike further away emotionally. Now, a solution had been worked out that was a win for both people. Fran could transfer most of her demands onto the professional caregivers at the home, and this allowed her to become closer to Mike, who in turn became a more sensitive and empathic son. As a result of these changes, Fran and Mike developed a more meaningful and loving relationship.

Creative solutions are always available. In order to find them, we must examine the processes that are in the way. Sometimes, professional consultation is helpful. Sometimes, struggling with the issues and trying to understand the other's point of view will do the trick. We must not let years go by while we remain embroiled in a morass. We must find, as Mike eventually did, the mechanisms that will allow us to free up and improve our relationship with our aged parents.

We have seen how attitudes can affect the process of aging negatively. There is a positive side as well. Before we discuss the story of an
individual who has maintained an optimistic attitude toward growing old,
let us consider some stories involving attitudes that are not only negative,
but bitter.

About five percent of the aged population in the United States
is institutionalized. Institutionalization occurs either because the elderly
parents are no longer capable of caring for themselves or because the
adult children wish to minimize their own responsibility. The most common medical conditions that leave the elderly unable to care for themselves are cancer, stroke, heart disease, and diabetes. Other illnesses that
can impair functioning include Alzheimer's disease, arthritis, emphysema,
osteoporosis, and Parkinson's disease. Several of these ailments may
coincide and overlap, and some are related to the formation of others, as
when hypertension leads to stroke. We must be aware of such disease processes so that we can help afflicted parents adapt. Any conditions that
require short-term, long-term, or permanent institutionalization have
special psychological dimensions, and call for a special awareness and
compassion.

Frank was 76 when he had a stroke. Before the stroke, he had lived
independently as a retired teacher. When he was younger, Frank had possessed a quick and at times violent temper. He drank and was often
involved in brawls. This changed when Frank was 42, after someone he
assaulted filed charges against him. Because it was a first offense, Frank was
not jailed, but his employer was informed and Frank came within a hair's
breadth of losing his job. After that, Frank labored to control his temper,
but his attitude remained one of pessimism and poor impulse control
throughout his life.

When Frank had the stroke, he was frightened that he would not
recover. After the shock wore off and his fear waned, he remained in a
state of depression and frustration for a long time. Rehabilitation was slow,
but effective enough that Frank could return to independent living after
about six months. His speech, which had been slurred, returned to normal, and his thought processes remained intact, though he occasionally
could not find the right word. Unfortunately, however, his right side was

partially paralyzed. He was unable to use his right arm at all, and he walked on his right leg with difficulty.

Frank reverted to the same attitude he had displayed as a young man. Whenever he was forced to confront his new disabilities, he became frustrated and violent. He complained bitterly to anyone who would listen. He rarely listened himself, but instead dominated conversations with his angry outpourings. His constant preoccupation with his condition, coupled with his lack of empathy for others, led Frank into an isolated life. Few people cared to spend time with him. His adult children found his attitude difficult to tolerate, but they saw that his basic needs were attended to. They hired someone to clean his apartment; his daughter pre-cooked his meals so that he only needed to microwave them; and they called him every day to see that he was all right. In short, they helped compensate for those things Frank could not perform on his own, but they rarely invited him to visit and never spent significant time with him. When family occasions took place, Frank was taken home at the earliest opportunity. You see, his children *loved* Frank and felt an obligation to assist him; however, they did not *like* him very much. While he had been a difficult but bearable person before the stroke, afterwards he had grown increasingly bitter and impossible to be around.

When Frank's son Mark first came to my office, his primary motivation for seeking counseling was guilt over neglecting his father's emotional needs. He was very articulate about how he did not like his father or the way his father behaved. Mark's dilemma involved finding a way to do the right thing without having to deal with his father's negativism. The solution was for Mark to explain to Frank's physician how Frank's attitude was hindering his full recovery. Frank's doctor put Frank on medications that altered his mood to the point where his children could participate less painfully in his life. Frank remained an irascible individual, but the extremes of his behavior were curtailed. Thus, his children were able to deal with him more rationally.

Frank, of course, would not consent to any sort of counseling, so I never had the opportunity to meet with him directly. I did, however, get the chance to help someone with a similar attitude adjust to his stroke-induced disabilities.

At age 74, Norman had a stroke that required him to be institutionalized. He could no longer make much use of his limbs on his right side. In addition, his speech was impaired. He had undergone rehabilitation, but his improvement had been impeded by his recalcitrance. Norman was very bitter and angry about his stroke, and he allowed these feelings to overcome his willingness to get better. Moreover, he displaced his rage onto the staff who were trying to help him regain function, as well as taking it out on his adult children, Mickey and Rhonda.

Norman managed to alienate almost everyone who tried to help him. He desperately wanted to function normally again, but he was so overwhelmed by his catastrophe that he was unable to respond in an accepting and cooperative manner. The difficulty he had speaking was especially frustrating, because he needed to express his fears and to release his feelings. In addition, Norman was embarrassed by the fact that his speech was badly slurred and that he often could not find words for his ideas. Few people were willing to put in the time and effort to get at his meaning, and those who did frequently witnessed Norman becoming angry, throwing objects, and cursing. You see, Norman knew what he wanted to say, but most of the time he had trouble getting it to come out. This made him furious, and his fury only made things worse. Because there were times when he was able to express himself adequately, people around him suspected that Norman was able to speak clearly, but willfully chose not to out of anger and bitterness. In fact, it was not his anger that caused his speech difficulty, but the other way around. Thus, Norman's predicament was usually misunderstood.

After a while, Norman was transferred to an extended care facility designed for people who were incapacitated, but did not need hospital care. Norman shared a dorm-style room with three other residents. The facility was rather stark, with little decoration and few amenities. Many residents took advantage of the dayroom, where they could watch television and interact with other residents and with staff. Organized programs such as crafts and concerts were offered, and college-age volunteers stopped by regularly to visit and chat. Norman's new home afforded a variety of opportunities to interact with others and have a life, but Norman remained isolated. He would not speak to anyone, and his angry attitude alienated many people. The volunteer assigned to him asked to be reassigned. Staff members interacted with him only when necessary, and his children visited less and less frequently. It seemed as if Norman were destined to spend the remainder of his life in isolation and bitterness.

Norman had worked as a skilled carpenter throughout most of his adult life. He had always worked with his hands. Quite early in his life, he had discovered his talent for building things, and he became an apprentice to a master carpenter. This man functioned as a surrogate father, mentor, and teacher to the young Norman. Norman's own father had deserted the family when Norman was a young boy. Norman had floundered for some time thereafter, becoming withdrawn and unsure of himself. Under the guidance of the master carpenter, however, Norman began to flourish. He discovered that he was capable of creating objects that were beautiful as well as useful, that he could express himself and release feelings in the medium of wood. He enjoyed listening to the praises of his clients when he finished a job. Because his self-esteem was linked to his projects, he never took shortcuts or gave less than expert workmanship. In time, he developed a reputation as a perfectionist who did superior work. When his mentor retired, Norman took over the business and carried on the tradition of master craftsmanship. Neither of his children showed an interest in carpentry. For a while, Norman had some apprentices working under him, but they were soon lured away by other carpenters who did not hold them to the exacting standards Norman did. Thus, Norman worked alone for an increasingly fewer number of clients who were seeking a higher standard of work and could afford to pay for it.

In his late sixties, Norman slowed down some, working only on jobs to which he was personally committed. When the stroke hit him, he was in the midst of building cabinets for a wealthy couple who were renovating a four-story mansion in the late Victorian style. This was Norman at his finest. He liked to think of himself as the peer of the carpenters of that era who had prided themselves on their design sensibility and fine craftsmanship. Alas, Norman's stroke prevented him from ever completing the job. This pained him greatly. In his isolation, he frequently thought about those cabinets and what he might have done if he had not been incapacitated. But such thoughts only further embittered his terrible isolation.

Norman was brought to my attention by a physician who tended to basic medical care at Norman's facility on a consultant basis. This physician routinely reviewed cases, treating the residents' simple medical conditions and making recommendations concerning their care and well-being. One day, he was called upon to treat a staff person who had been punched in the face by a resident. The resident, of course, was Norman. Norman had become so frustrated that he had assaulted the staff member. His hands, once used to express creativity, now expressed rage.

This incident led to a discussion about Norman's appropriateness for the facility. It was agreed that if Norman continued to be combative, he would have to be transferred or medicated. Fortunately for Norman, the physician was a sensitive, inquisitive person. He investigated Norman's case. As he did so, he wondered about Norman's motivation. He could imagine how, under similar life circumstances, he, too, might feel like striking out. This empathic identification with Norman led the physician to request a consultation with me. I was asked to evaluate Norman to see what sort of treatment plan might help staff deal with him, or whether a transfer to a more controlled environment was required.

First, I met with the staff. They explained to me how belligerent Norman was, using quite graphic terms. It became clear that many of them were angry at Norman. Some focused on his uncooperativeness, others on his negative predisposition in virtually any interaction. Even those who had only minimal contact with Norman had developed a strongly negative perception of him. The attitude of the staff was monumentally negative; clearly, they had given up on Norman and were lobbying for his transfer. I wondered how such intensity could be modified in the interest of a therapeutic treatment plan, or if it could be. These people, otherwise helpful and compassionate individuals, seemed irremediably hostile to Norman, and I wondered how anyone, no less a debilitated elderly stroke victim, could possibly thrive under such conditions.

I first observed Norman interacting with staff in the dayroom. It became apparent why the staff felt as they did. Norman snapped at them and reacted negatively to any encounter. He mostly looked at the floor, rarely made eye contact, and mumbled unintelligible phrases with his teeth clenched in an intensely angry fashion. I knew that this man could not possibly be happy with his life as it existed. In all likelihood, he sought the same things we all want – friendship, a feeling of connectedness, a sense of having an impact on the world around us. I could only conclude that Norman was as frustrated and angry as the staff. Norman took his feelings out on the staff, and the staff reacted by taking their feelings out on Norman. In fact, they were all frustrated with the situation as it existed, and they projected their feelings reciprocally onto each other.

Next, I spent some time with Norman alone. He was belligerent, so I elected to return for short visits over several days. In these meetings, I asked him simple questions and labored hard to understand his answers. Frequently, I made statements like, "I am trying as hard as I know how to comprehend what you are saying. I know it is frustrating for you not to be understood, but let's not give up. You are important, and I want to keep trying." When he got angry because I was unable to follow him, I would reflect back his obvious feeling: "I can see you are angry and upset." Even if I did not get the point of what he was saying, I was in some small way understanding his emotional experience and connecting with him. I also reflected back what I thought might be going on inside him. For example, I might say, "It must be very painful to be so isolated and to feel so alone," to which Norman might respond with a head nod. Sometimes, when I identified certain feeling states, or when I talked about what it must have been like to have his life disrupted so suddenly, Norman would get tears in his eyes. Sometimes, I would tell him a joke, and he would smile. Once, I sought his advice about a carpentry project I was considering, and Norman imparted a little of his expertise. In short, Norman and I began to relate, and our relationship provided a model for the staff of how to interact and connect with Norman.

Norman began to look forward to my visits. His behavior had changed just enough so that the staff could recognize a difference and develop an interest in what I was doing. Each time I met with Norman, I also met separately with the staff. I allowed them to vent their frustrations, and I began to share what was happening in my conversations with Norman. I also emphasized the tragic proportions of Norman's dilemma. As the staff listened, they began to change their view of this man. They stopped seeing him as a problem patient and began to understand him as a human being who was reacting to the pain and distress of losing his lifestyle, his independence, his mobility, and even his ability to communicate. Though the stroke had affected his functioning, Norman was still a person inside, and he needed to connect with others, perhaps more than he ever had before.

As Norman's humanness emerged and the staff came to understand him more completely, their compassion for him grew. They became willing to change the pattern of negative interaction by learning new methods of relating. I trained several staff members how to work with Norman's particular difficulty. This training consisted of both discussion and role playing, in which one staff member pretended to be Norman while the other would practice relating to him. In time, these staff members joined my sessions with Norman, at first observing how I related to him and later trying it out themselves. As this process gained momentum, the staff actually began to look forward to interacting with Norman. As a result, Norman's behavior improved significantly. He rarely got angry. When he did, the staff could help him express and defuse his feelings. He became cooperative and much more interactive. He even revealed a sense of humor!

Thus, the destructive interactive pattern that had developed between Norman and the staff was replaced by a positive pattern, resulting in a better quality of life for Norman. Both sides came to understand each other because the staff had made an extra effort to see the person behind the behavior and to learn appropriate methods of relating to him. A lose-lose situation was now a mutually rewarding one. This example should be taken to heart by those of us whose aged parents have had a stroke or are in some significant way debilitated. When our parents are institutionalized, we must carefully observe the relational patterns that evolve as they interact with staff. If the patterns seem to be destructive, some sort of modification must be instituted at once. Norman's story also teaches a more universal lesson. *If we try to understand what life is like for our aged parents, we will be better equipped to act on their behalf.*

It is always expedient to consider the interactive patterns that exist between our aged parents and other significant people in their lives. For example, we might accompany our parents to their next doctor visit to see if that relationship enjoys free and full communication. Commonly, the elderly are reluctant to discuss certain issues if a member of the opposite sex is in the room; hence, a medical student observing a physician teacher can inadvertently impede communication. A busy doctor may exit the room before an aged parent has been able to bring up information about a specific medical concern. We must not allow these important details to escape our notice. If we observe carefully, we can facilitate communication between our parents and the other people they depend on for help. Do not be like Norman's children, Mickey and Rhonda, who left their father's well-being in the hands of fate. They were fortunate that Norman wound up with a physician who understood how attitude and motivation were intertwined with health, a physician who made an effort to identify empathically with Norman. We should not expect to be so lucky.

Let us now turn to the story of Milly, a 75-year-old stroke victim who maintained a positive attitude and was thus able to transcend her incapacities. Milly lived alone in a small one-story house about five blocks from her 55-year-old daughter, Jean. After the stroke, Milly made enough of a recovery that she was able to return to her home and take care of herself with only modest assistance from Jean. Milly's mobility was affected by the stroke. She was unsteady on her feet, but she could walk with the aid of a three-pronged cane and at times used a walker. She could get in and out of a car, so she could accompany Jean on trips to the grocery store or the mall; if she became tired there, she used a motorized cart. Milly's speech was also affected, though not nearly as dramatically as Norman's. Milly sometimes slurred her words or was unable to come up with a particular word that was central to what she was trying to say. If listened to with a little patience, however, she could be understood.

Milly received counseling throughout her recovery, and this helped her to maintain her positive attitude. By nature, she was an easygoing person and, despite her age, very adaptive and optimistic. She had shown this throughout her life. When her husband died ten years earlier, she mourned his death for some time; still, she managed to forge a new life that was quite active and meaningful. After the stroke, she again showed this ability to roll with the punches and make the best of things. Of course, Milly experienced frustration when she had difficulty speaking.

She observed that many people equated her slow, labored speech with lack of intelligence. "People think I'm stupid because of the way I talk," she told me once. "They figure, because my speech is damaged, my mind must be damaged, too. They often talk to me like I'm a baby or something. They speak loudly as if my hearing were bad, but it isn't. They become impatient when I can't come up with a word. Sometimes, they even cut me off, like what I'm trying to say isn't important. They placate me, and I find that demeaning. Even some of my friends refuse to treat me like an adult. I used to play cards with five other women. After my stroke, they let me know pretty quickly that I should not come back to the card group. I understand; they think I can't play well because my speech is bad. But I can. I'm the same person I always was. Inside, I'm still me."

Milly understood how she was perceived by most other people. She was hurt that many of the people she thought of as friends had deserted her when she needed them, but she did not remain angry and resentful. Instead, she expressed her feelings and moved on. This is a sign of emotional maturity. It is also further evidence of Milly's adaptability and optimism. Milly is going to survive and thrive. She will forge a new life and find new people to relate to and be with. Her therapy facilitated this process, and also served as a place where Milly and Jean could discuss their concerns about one another and their relationship. Initially, Jean had also treated her mother like a child, but when Milly explained how demeaning this was, Jean changed her behavior at once. In the end, Jean adapted to her mother's limitations and came to understand all her difficulties, and this allowed mother and daughter to maintain an open, communicative relationship. Jean and Milly take into account the effects of Milly's stroke, and neither allows the stroke to hurt their relationship.

It is possible to adjust to our parents' gradually increasing debilities in an open and loving manner. To do this, we must recognize the extent of their limitations, and we must take pains to be accurate in our assessment. We must not mistake a change in our parents' functioning for an irrevocable alteration in who they are or what they are in relation to us. A process of evaluation and reevaluation is required. It can be useful to explore the more difficult issues with an impartial third party, someone who can facilitate the communication process and augment understanding. Do not be afraid to use such a professional, especially if you have a sense that communication is breaking down. It is important to remember Milly's simply stated and eloquent point: no matter what had changed in the way she spoke or functioned, she was still the same person inside. Our aged parents' circumstances may have altered, their physical condition may be different, their thought processes may have slowed down, their ability to communicate may be impaired, and their ideas and feelings may have changed, but they remain and always will remain people inside, people who have a full range of emotional and intellectual responses. We must not fall into the trap of seeing them as less expressive or less complex than we are. If we do this, we skew our perceptions and diminish our ability to know and understand them. This can only demean both us and them and interfere with meaningful and important interactive relating.

Let us now turn to the story of an elderly person who displays a positive attitude about the aging process itself. At 90, Oliver is intellectually and physically largely the person he has always been. He has aged with grace and wisdom. His story provides a splendid example of how a positive outlook and an adaptive attitude can enable us to grow and thrive throughout our lives.

Let me begin by describing his current weekly routines. On Monday, Wednesday, and Friday, Oliver plays golf with three partners whom he has known for decades. While all four men are retired, Oliver is the eldest by many years. He plays between 12 and 18 holes. Age has required him to make some accommodations, of course. Though he once had excellent eyesight, he now has difficulty tracking his shots and must rely on one of his companions to assist him. His tee shots are not as long as they once were, so he uses a new club which provides more distance and accuracy. He has also adjusted his expectations. He knows he will never again shoot in the eighties, but he does not let his declining performance interfere with the pleasure he gets from playing the game.

On Tuesday, he goes downtown for breakfast, to a coffee shop that many of his old friends in the New York City garment center frequent. His closest friend, also a retired salesman, meets him there, and they socialize for a while with the current crop of salespeople. After a couple of hours, he and his friend go off and engage in some other activity.

Sometimes, they go to lectures at the New York Public Library. Sometimes, they attend outdoor concerts in Bryant Park. Sometimes, they just stroll the streets of Manhattan. Occasionally, the two visit the old neighborhood on the Lower East Side where they grew up.

On Thursday, Oliver takes care of any errands he may have and goes for a long walk. He has mapped out a particular route that he enjoys, and he usually follows it. These excursions have been part of his life for many years. He began to walk daily after the first articles on the benefits of exercise appeared, and he has done so ever since. Likewise, the first anti-smoking articles in the 1940s inspired him to quit smoking. When he read about the benefits of a low-fat diet and of staying trim, he adjusted his lifestyle accordingly. On weekends, he also walks and, being an avid sports fan, he watches various sporting events (especially golf, his favorite) on television. Interspersed in this routine are visits from children, grand-children, and neighbors. In sum, Oliver leads an active and meaningful life.

Much of his success stems from his attitude. Oliver has always been a pragmatist. He assesses a situation, draws a conclusion, and then follows through with his decision. When it became apparent that his golf game was worsening, instead of getting upset, he evaluated why. It seemed that his upper body strength had diminished as a result of aging. As soon as he figured this out, he came up with an exercise plan which involved low-poundage hand weights, and he proceeded to follow it religiously. As a result, his game improved. When his wife died several years ago, Oliver was left alone not only in his grief, but also with some significant practical problems. For example, his wife had done the cooking for all of their 60-year marriage, and Oliver was suddenly forced to fend for himself in an area in which he had no experience. Characteristically, however, he set about reading cookbooks and learning how to prepare basic dishes, using his neighbors and his children as consultants, and now he can cook a variety of foods. Here, then, was a man in his late eighties who had never cooked for himself suddenly forced to do so. So he does! He adapts to the situation and meets the challenge pragmatically.

This sort of behavior is typical of Oliver. He has never shied away from difficult decisions; instead, he accepts the realities before him, evaluates them, and does what he needs to do. He uses his resources well and is not afraid to ask for help when he needs it. His attitude toward the aging process is no different. A few years ago, having recognized that the time would soon come when he could no longer live independently, he moved into an apartment at a facility that offers a continuum of care, ranging from minimally supervised housing to full nursing home care within the same complex. He can cook for himself or eat communally, do his own laundry or have it done, clean his apartment or have it cleaned, partake in social events or be as reclusive as he chooses. Moreover, the facility is near to where he used to live, so none of his routines were disrupted. Thus, Oliver has anticipated and prepared for his eventual decline; he has arranged to have the resources, as he needs them, to adapt to it over time; and he has made choices that accord with his tastes and predilections, so that he might hold on to his pleasures and maximize the quality of his life.

Oliver's example clearly shows the power of attitude to affect the quality of life during the aging process. If you find that your own elderly parents have not done so well, do not become discouraged. Your attitude can be equally important, and you can take steps to help your parents improve theirs, as we have seen. If you find yourself becoming frustrated and disheartened, look upon these feelings as a *phase* that you may need to pass through in order to reach a level of realistic acceptance that will enable you to find creative solutions. If you have trouble pulling out of this phase, do not be afraid to seek professional counsel. It is always wiser to seek help than to continue feeling pessimistic about the potential for change. Psychologists, social workers, priests, rabbis, ministers, geriatric specialists, nurses, and doctors all have the expertise and the resources to help you come up with a successful mechanism to turn things around. After all, if your attitude is pessimistic, how can you possibly be in a position to help your aged parents?

Of course, you must be realistic in your expectations. You cannot expect 80-year-olds with acute arthritic deterioration to go to a dance. But perhaps you can realistically encourage them to take a movement class of some sort. Many care facilities offer such classes, specifically designed for the elderly. Also, do not neglect to consider the wonders that our technological age affords. One hundred years ago, a hearing-impaired person faced an insurmountable obstacle in trying to lead a socially interactive existence.

Today, a hearing aid can overcome this impediment, though the need for such intervention sometimes goes unnoticed and the aged parent may require a great deal of encouragement to employ such a device. Such advances are becoming commonplace, and technologies become quickly available to those in need. Keep abreast of such developments. A new technology might produce a significant improvement in your aged parents' quality of life.

We began this chapter by looking at biological and psychological aspects of the aging process. Biology and psychology are two broad categories that should be constantly in our awareness as we relate to our aged parents and participate in ensuring their quality of life. Some things we have little control over, but we always have the ability to intervene, plan, and help our aged parents adapt emotionally to whatever circumstances they must face. In addition, we can weigh these circumstances against their attitudes about life and, in doing so, get a sense of how and whether their attitude helps their position or hinders it. If their attitude affects them positively, we can take steps to facilitate it; if it is detrimental, we can consider how to help our aged parents make psychological changes that allow for a more meaningful and rewarding life. Regardless of the biological and circumstantial picture, attitude can be modified at any age.

Our task, then, is one of *awareness,* awareness of all the complex and intertwining factors that affect our parents as they age. Only through awareness can we find the means of intervention that will enhance their quality of life. In order to be aware, however, we must also be self-aware; we must understand our own complex emotions and learn how to compensate for any distortions these may produce. Only then will we be able to help our aged parents to live out their lives in a meaningful, growing, and adaptive manner.

My mother's attitude remained consistent throughout her life. She maintained a sweet and cooperative and optimistic perspective, no matter what she faced.

I can remember when she was diagnosed with breast cancer. It was clear that the malignancy was growing and spreading. She was, of course, initially shocked when she heard the news. Anyone facing such a serious affliction is shaken, afraid, and worried about the future. All other issues become secondary, as considerable mental and physical energies become focused on what may be a life and death struggle.

Breast cancer is an especially difficult condition, for it involves the possibility of mastectomy, and many sufferers become distraught over the prospect. My mother had a friend who refused to undergo such a surgery, against the advice of her doctors and despite her children's pleas. When this friend was diagnosed several years earlier, my mother sought to help her. Unlike many others whose fear of such a fate made them avoid the friend as if she were contagious, my mother responded to her friend's condition in a supportive way. This was part of her personality structure: she simply never considered another response. My mother visited her friend often. She did not tell her what to do; she listened to her fears and, in effect, nurtured her. This particular woman simply could not face the fact that a mastectomy was the best form of treatment in her situation. She refused to even consider it and, instead, opted for other treatments, such as radiation and chemotherapy. My mother faithfully supported her friend through these treatments, which prolonged the length of her life, but impaired its quality. My mother was horrified to watch her once vibrant friend slowly deteriorate, but she stayed near her bedside. In the end, the treatments were in vain, and the woman died. Despite the sadness and horror of the situation, my mother remained true. She helped her friend to bear the disease and the treatments, and to approach her death, with dignity.

My mother recognized that this agonizing death could have been the result of her friend's choice not to have her breasts surgically removed, and she did not forget this painful lesson. Thus, when she found herself in the same dilemma, she knew immediately what needed to be done. She was able to articulate her thinking and to face the surgery, not just with resolution, but with courage. She directly stated that she wanted to live and that she would do whatever it took to survive. I can remember her saying, "Davey, don't get me wrong. I like my breast, and I don't want to lose it. But if it is a choice between keeping my breast and living, I can do without my breast." It was clear in her mind that her goal was to survive the cancer and that she would take whatever path led in that direction. She had watched her friend make a different choice and die. She would not let that happen to herself, so she had the mastectomy. She knew what needed to be done and did it. As a result, she was able to live another 15 years. She never looked back or regretted her decision. I never once heard her complain about how life had dealt her a bad blow or that she had lost a body part highly valued in our society. Instead, she felt that she made the best decision possible, and she proceeded optimistically and realistically with her life.

A short while before my mother's death, I joined her and my father in a walk around the neighborhood. We were strolling down the block on a nice spring day. The sun was out and everything looked green and alive. My father was holding my mother's hand as we walked, and I was at her other side. By then, her heart disease had progressed, and she was suffering from Alzheimer's disease. She frequently lost her train of thought and became confused. She often repeated herself, asking the same questions over and over, losing the answer again and again. "How are the kids?" she would ask me, and I would answer, but a few moments later she would ask again. "How are the kids?" It was as if she knew she wanted to find out something important, but in the complex interweaving of nerve bundles the answer was lost. She was left with the same feeling that motivated the question, so she would ask it once again unaware that she had already been given an answer.

By then, this was the pattern of her interactions most of the time. We had to be patient as well as sensitive to her plight. On our walk that day, the same exchange occurred perhaps 10 times in the course of 20 minutes. Each time, I painstakingly tried to answer her. My father helped me, trying to remind her of what I had told her only moments before. Once, however, he became annoyed and scolded her. "He already answered you five times. Just drop it." She was hurt by his response because, from her point of view, there was no reason to get angry. I remember her telling me, "Your father must be getting old. He gets irritable and snappy so often." The irony of her statements did not escape me. More importantly, however, I came to realize that, although my mother could not remember what any of us said from one moment to the next, she could still sense a pattern of negative emotional responses. Here was this sweet woman, excusing my father's harshness toward her by blaming it on his age! Of course, it was her repetitiveness, which he usually endured with unremitting tolerance, that on this occasion caused him to lose his patience and react negatively. As I glanced over at my mother, I saw the woman who had raised and loved me. In a sense, she looked as she had always looked. Yes, she looked older and more worn, but her face still showed the effects of a lifetime of positive perspective. She did not appear angry or bitter; there were no worry lines in her face, only smile lines. She remained, even in this state, a gentle, positive, optimistic, and sweet person.

It is hard to think of her and not conjure up those words. I have used them many times as I have written about her. This is not the result of some literary oversight — no, these are the right words to describe her. It was very clear as we strolled *around the block together that, despite my mother's incessant questions and inability to retain our answers, my father and I shared a deep love for her. Above all, we knew that we would sacrifice almost anything to help her be content and happy in her life. When my father looked at my mother, I could tell that he did not see her as an old woman whose mind was damaged, whose face was wrinkled, and whose body was frail and scarred. Instead, he saw her inner beauty, her sensitivity and nurturance, her good and gentle nature, her loyal and stalwart support for others, her kind heart and her selflessness. I remember him gazing upon her and saying, "You know, Dave, your mother is still the most beautiful woman I know." He said these words with absolute sincerity. He saw beyond the ravages she had suffered; indeed, he saw that her finest qualities could not be ravaged. He related to who she was and always had been, not what she looked like. And he was right to do so.*

CHAPTER FIVE

WHEN WE LOSE THEM

Up to this point, we have focused on the first good-bye, on our parents' gradual deterioration and the need for us to recognize and respond to it. In this chapter, we will look at the second good-bye, at the experience of losing our parents to death.

For most of us, this is a terribly distasteful topic. We love our aged parents, and few of us can face the eventuality of their death on an emotional level, no matter how well we might understand it intellectually. Facing our parents' death forces us to confront some very difficult issues. For one thing, our parents' death means that we will lose the feeling of having support at all times and in all circumstances. This dimension of loss seems to be an important factor in all but the most dysfunctional parent-child relationships. For as long as we can remember, our parents have been there to help us through the hard times. If we suffered a loss, they consoled us; if we experienced financial problems, they helped us out; if our marriages ended, they were there to get us through the pain; if we lost our jobs, they encouraged us to regroup. In short, they stood by us, and we knew that they were always there when we needed them. As our parents aged, their ability to help us may have been compromised; nevertheless, we could still find reassurance in their loving presence, and in the memories of support and security that it conjured up.

With death, however, that presence is gone, absolutely and irrevocably. Our parents are no longer there, and we are left with only the memory of their unconditional support. It is not that we lack the skills to get through our troubles ourselves, or that we have not developed other support systems to help us in difficult times. Indeed, most of us are competent individuals who have friends and resources to draw on during such periods. Rather, it is that we have lost a fundamental presence in our lives, a presence which, up to this point, we have never been without. Perhaps we took our parents for granted or did not think of ourselves as dependent on them, but when they are suddenly gone, when we have a growing recognition that they will never be with us again, that we must now live our lives without them – only then do we realize that their very presence was an important emotional support.

The death of our parents also makes us aware that there has been a shift in the cycle of life. We are now becoming our children's aging parents, and we assume this role bereft of our strongest and most lasting support. The resulting feeling of insecurity and helplessness heightens our sense that our own death is imminent, that our parents' death foretells our own. This realization is unnerving, and many of us do what we can to deny and avoid it.

The emotional aftermath of our parents' death can also be traumatic. We are disoriented and confused; we are dazed and unanchored. We may experience difficulty sleeping or concentrating on tasks. Often, there is a sense of unreality: we may go through our routine – get up, brush our teeth, take a shower, go to work, go home, make dinner, and so on – but we go through the motions mechanically, without feeling a part of anything we are involved in.

This is a period of adjustment. During this period, we are moving from a sense of shock at death to a functional reality in which we do what we have to do, but we feel detached from our actions and estranged from the buzz and commotion of life. In time, however, we come to accept our loss; we once again rejoin the world as full participants. We do not forget our parents. We continue to miss them at times, such as on the anniversaries of their deaths or at family celebrations, and we especially miss them during crises, when their support and guidance would have been helpful. Nonetheless, in time there is a shift, often a subtle one, from grieving for the loss to remembering our parents fondly and reminiscing about things they did and said.

For some, this transition happens easily. For others, it may take longer. There is no way to predict the course of this painful process, but you should not underestimate its impact. Having supportive people available is very helpful, of course, but supporting a grieving person is a task many people misunderstand. It is not uncommon for friends, spouses, and children to rally around a bereaved person for a few days or perhaps a few weeks, but then to withdraw or communicate in one way or another that they no longer wish to hear about the loss. Usually, such people mean well; they simply do not understand the depth of the loss, and therefore cannot understand the intensity of the need or the duration of the pain. Unfortunately, however, this behavior has the impact of a second loss. First, the adult child loses a parent to death; later, he is emotionally abandoned by those closest to him.

Many people equate being functional with being over grief. They may think that you no longer feel sad and upset if you can do your job and live up to your responsibilities competently. When people around you believe you are done grieving, you may become reluctant to open up your feelings for fear that you will be considered weak. This is a mistake. It takes strength to let your needs be known. If you want the support of your friends, be open about it. Let them know how you feel and what you are going through. If you cannot do this, consider writing about how you feel. Try writing a letter to the parent you have lost, or start a journal about your grieving process. In some communities, there are support groups for people in various stages of grieving. Professional counseling is another route to resolution. No matter where you turn for help in resolving your grief, try to remember that you are going through a painful but normal developmental stage, and do whatever you need to do to get through it. Your way may not resemble the path a friend took; grieving is a different experience for each one of us. Find the method that works best for you.

You will probably feel guilt after the death of your parent, and in some instances this is a justified feeling. I am reminded of a friend who lived in a suburban community about 60 miles away from his octogenarian father. This fellow always sent his father cards and gifts when appropriate, but he would visit his father only rarely. His father had a quirk – he always declined invitations to visit his son's home. He would say, "What am I going to do there? I have everything here." What he meant, of course, was that he felt secure in his home and neighborhood, and to spend a week or more in an unfamiliar environment was a threatening prospect. His son, my friend, had trouble reading between the lines. When his father turned down his invitations, he came away feeling frustrated and hurt. "I don't understand him. He could enjoy this beautiful house, and do everything he does at home, and still be around family. And he just won't do it," he complained. Naturally, in time his offers became less frequent, and eventually they stopped altogether.

The son interpreted his father's behavior as a rejection of his lifestyle and of himself. He failed to realize how, like many elderly people, his father was so embedded in his routines that leaving them made him feel anxious and unsafe. It was within the son's power to focus on the larger issues, such as the need to care for his father and to maintain a link between his father and his own children; instead, however, he allowed his feeling of rejection to get in the way. He rarely visited his father, even when he was in the area for business or to take his children to a nearby cultural event. He rationalized his behavior by telling himself, "We won't have time" or "We might interfere with his plans."

In truth, he avoided contact with his father so that he could avoid encountering the terribly painful rejection he perceived. I say *perceived* because it was not clear that rejection was intended; more likely, his father simply wished to remain where he felt most secure. Because the son perceived rejection, he put a significant distance and an emotionally protective barrier between his father and himself. This prevented him from bonding with this father in a way that might have been meaningful to both of them.

Unfortunately, the father died, and the son was left to face the consequences of his behavior. Even though he had kept his distance while his father was alive, he had always had a vague and unspoken feeling that somehow, someday, their estrangement would change. Now, it never could. Thus, the son had to face great remorse and guilt as well as loss. Why hadn't he spent more time with his father? How could he have been so foolish as to not connect with his father when he had had the chance? In retrospect, it was clear to him that he should have acted to change the situation. Instead, to avoid brushing against perceived rejection, he had steered clear of his father; as a result, he and his father had forever lost the opportunity to resolve their issues and renew their relationship, and he had robbed his own children of meaningful interactions with their grandfather.

To some extent, we all are left with insoluble issues and guilt when our parents die. There is always something we wish we had done. "Why didn't I call her when I thought about it the night before she died?" "Why didn't I give him a more meaningful present on his last birthday?" "Why didn't I tell her I loved her?" "Why didn't I bring the kids to see him more often?" "Why didn't I send her on that trip she always wanted to take?"

Such self-recriminations are common. Objectively speaking, many of these are minor transgressions. Sometimes, however, there are things we learn only after the death of our parents that we wish we had known about and responded to beforehand. For example, at the funeral, one of your parent's friends might reveal how much your parent enjoyed the theater. You might say to yourself, "How did I miss this important detail about my parent's life? If I had known, we could have gone together. I could have given him tickets for Christmas and for his birthday." Or, worse, perhaps you learn that your parent had confided to a friend that he was unhappy about some important aspect of his living arrangements or the care he was receiving, but he did not want to bother you about it. You might ask yourself, "Why didn't I figure out how he felt about this? How could I have been too busy to notice something so important? Why didn't I draw him out more? Why did I allow my absorption in my own problems to detract from the attention I should have been giving to him?"

I am reminded of my neighbor, Ric, who went to visit his old neighborhood not long after his mother's death. While walking around, he chanced upon a woman who had been a close friend of his mother's. Over coffee, the friend revealed that, for a number of years, Ric's mother had been deeply hurt by her other son's behavior. Ric's brother was a successful businessman who frequently traveled the globe. Ric's mother was hurt that this wealthy son never once brought her a souvenir from his travels. It was not that she wanted him to give her gifts. Rather, she simply wanted to know that her son remembered her. Because he was away so much, she saw him infrequently, and she needed to be reassured that she was important to him. She thought that he was embarrassed by her lack of sophistication, and she told her friend how distressed it made her feel to think so. Ric felt dumbfounded at hearing about his mother's feelings. He had noticed that there was an emotional estrangement between his mother and his brother, and he knew how self-centered his brother was, but he never suspected the depth of his mother's pain.

Afterwards, Ric was troubled for a long time. He felt guilty that he had not been more aware of his mother's suffering. He was angry at himself for not recognizing this aspect of his mother's life. Had he known of it, he might have acted to correct it, or at least he might have helped his mother deal with her feelings. His mother, of course, had not confided in him because she did not want to burden him with her troubles. She also was afraid that telling Ric would create a rift between the brothers, and she wanted her sons to take care of each other after she was gone. Thus, out of love and protectiveness, she had spared Ric her pain, and now, after her death, Ric knows about it and feels intensely guilty.

Guilt is something all of us encounter after our aged parents die. It seems to be part of the transition we go through. No matter how attentive we have been to our parents, regardless of how much we have done to help them, we experience remorse for not having noticed or done more. Of course, the guilt is much more intense if we really have failed in significant ways.

For those of us who attempted to be loving, caring, responsive children, the guilt is often about things we could not or did not do for solid reasons, such as geographical distances, financial restraints, or pardonable ignorance. The guilt is present because we are not perfect, and therefore our response to our aged parents can never be complete. There will always be, to a greater or lesser extent, things undone, and we have to develop a perspective that takes this into account. In short, we have to forgive ourselves for being human. We can do no more than we are capable of doing, and we can respond to needs only if we recognize those needs. Self-reproach after the death of a parent seems to be almost universal, however. Thus, we should accept it as a part of our experience, recognize it when it occurs, and try to pass through it as quickly and painlessly as possible. You may feel inclined to keep these feelings secret, but you should not. Seek a trusted confidante or a professional listener. It is always easier to resolve your feelings if you express them.

There is one other aspect of guilt that must be mentioned. When our parents die, there is often a feeling of relief that a long-anticipated end has come. A sense of freedom arises from no longer having to face the eventuality and from the fact that we ourselves are still alive and able to resume a normal existence. Such relief is attended by guilt feelings, and these guilt feelings become more acute when friends and relatives have trouble understanding what we are going through. It is easier and more acceptable to show our relief if our parents have died of a protracted illness. In such circumstances, when we say we are glad that the suffering is over, we mean our parents' suffering and then our own, and this response is usually met with sympathy and understanding. If our parents die with little or no suffering, however, expressing relief feels inappropriate. To admit that we feel freed from burdensome responsibilities and from worrying about the future violates our own sense of the proper response and is considered ghoulish and unacceptable by those who cannot relate. Do not get caught up in worrying about the correctness of your feelings. Talk about them with someone you trust, someone who has been through a similar experience or who will make an extra effort to understand you. Otherwise, the difficulty you are facing will only worsen.

The story of Anna illustrates this point. Anna had cared for her elderly father for several years. She spoke to him daily and, since he lived nearby, she visited several times a week, often cooking his meals and cleaning his apartment. Her father took it for granted that she should do this. He came from a generation in which extended family often lived together and took care of one another. In fact, when Anna was a child, her grandmother had lived with the family. The grandmother had moved in after her husband's death, and Anna's parents had tended to her needs until she died. Hence, there was a tradition of caring for the elderly in Anna's family.

However, Anna's uncles and aunts, who also lived nearby, helped her parents with the caretaking. They had their mother over for dinner, they took her on vacations or into their homes for extended periods, and they contributed financially whenever they could. Thus, there was tremendous support and shared commitment. By the time it was Anna's turn to care for her father, however, the situation was entirely different. Her uncles and aunts had passed on, and her cousins had moved away. The old family closeness no longer existed.

Anna had remained in the old neighborhood near her father, but her two brothers had moved, one to a suburb two hours away, the other to a distant state. While both brothers helped their father financially, neither was present for day-to-day support. Anna was forced to take on virtually all of the caretaking. When there was an emergency and she had to make a quick decision about her father's medical treatment, there was not enough time to seek input from her brothers. This made the brothers angry, and they would criticize Anna for not seeking their counsel as well as for making the wrong decision.

As Anna's father came to require more of her time, Anna had less time and energy for herself. She had to stop going to night classes because her father needed her to prepare his dinner. She began to date less often because she rarely had the opportunity to go out and meet people. After all, she worked full-time, managed two houses, and helped her father with everything, from handling his finances to getting to his doctor's appointments. Gradually, Anna's life became increasingly overburdened, yet she felt she had no other choice. In her view, she was doing what a responsible adult child should do.

In fact, Anna was doing too much. There were resources in the community that could have relieved her of some of her responsibilities; however, like many of us, Anna became so embedded in what she felt she had to do that she could not imagine the alternatives.

In the end, her father died of a heart attack one afternoon as he watched a baseball game on television. Anna experienced the aftermath the way many of us do, with a combination of disbelief, sadness, confusion, depression, anger, and guilt. But Anna's guilt was intensified by her sense of relief that the burden of caring for her father was now lifted. Her life had been on hold for so long; perhaps now she could get it back. Yet how could she reconcile her relief at her father's death with her grief at his loss?

This contradiction tormented Anna. In the weeks after her father's death, she found herself feeling guilty every time she engaged in one of the pleasurable activities which, before her father's death, her duties had prohibited. As time progressed, this guilt came to inhibit her action, and she found herself becoming isolated and withdrawn. She attributed her reclusiveness to her grief over the loss of her beloved father. This, of course, was only partly true. Anna withdrew from life because enjoying life made her feel like she had not loved her father enough.

Anna was too embarrassed to talk about these feelings. If she tried to describe her guilt, she was immediately forced to confront its source, and if she acknowledged feeling relieved by her father's death, she proved herself a bad daughter. What listener, upon hearing of her relief, would not think her cold-blooded and cruel? Thus, she kept her feelings to herself. But isolation only made Anna's condition worse. Because she did not air her feelings, they began to fester.

Finally, Anna sought professional intervention. In treatment, she was able to discuss her feelings openly. As she came to understand her conflict, she began to free herself of the immobilizing influence of her perception of the situation. She began to realize that her feelings were not unacceptable, but rather human and OK to have. She was not a monster who had responded shamefully to her father's death, but a person who felt all of the normal complex feelings that accompany the death of a parent, including guilt and relief. Moreover, she felt relief from the burden of her father's care, not relief at his death, so she had no reason to be ashamed of it. In fact, she had done more than right by her father. By openly expressing her emotions and working through them with her therapist, Anna was able to resume her life, free of her guilt over this aspect of her father's death. She was able to develop a realistic view herself as a human being who had responded normally to a difficult situation, not as a bad daughter who should punish herself with deprivation.

We must all be aware of this dimension of the grief process. Do not be afraid to seek help from a professional if there is no one else for you to talk to, or if you do not feel safe sharing your confidences with family members or friends, or if you become unable to resolve your difficulties on your own. It is important to express the complex and often ambivalent feelings that arise during this painful and significant period in our lives.

Death is an inescapable fact of life. All of us will die, and all of our loved ones will die. This is difficult to think about. Interestingly, however, though many of us spend considerable time and energy contemplating death, we avoid doing the very thing that might alleviate some of the fear and perturbation surrounding it; that is, we avoid talking about it. Many of us feel that discussing our anxieties, no matter what the subject, means revealing our emotional weakness. Nothing could be more false or more self-defeating. In reality, it requires a great deal of strength and courage to speak openly, especially about our worst fears. Most people will respond with sensitivity to a confession of fear or anxiety about death, simply because they are in the same *human* predicament and therefore can empathize with you. These issues are universal – yet the reluctance to discuss them also seems to be universal!

At least, this was the case until 1969, when a book was published that had an enormous impact on both the professional world and the consciousness of the public at large. This book, *On Death and Dying* by Elizabeth Kübler-Ross, was immediately recognized as a landmark work. Kübler-Ross was, at that time, a practicing psychiatrist. Her practice brought her into contact with many people who were dying. She astutely observed these people's responses to the process as well as how they were treated by family, friends, clergy, physicians, and institutions. She then formulated a clear and highly useful framework by which the whole process of death and dying could be understood.

Kübler-Ross describes five stages that people who are dying pass through: *denial, anger, bargaining, depression,* and *acceptance.* Finally, there is death. These stages are not all-inclusive. Some people pass through all five of them, while others skip some and still others become stuck at one stage. Nevertheless, these five stages allow us to approach a dying person's experience with greater understanding. When most of us encounter a loved one who is dying, we do not know how to understand what is happening to him psychologically, particularly since we have our own fears about the process. Kübler-Ross's five stages provide a model that allows us to anticipate how our dying loved ones will behave, at least in general terms, and teaches us how to view their behavior as expressions of the dying process. This model also helps us to recognize when our loved ones are stuck at a particular stage, and therefore enables us to help them move on so that process of dying can be freer.

Let us examine these five stages more closely. *Denial* is the first stage. Denial is a defensive psychological process that we employ to protect ourselves from issues that seem overwhelming. It is a means of relieving ourselves of the fear and anxiety associated with intense negative experiences. When people are told they have a terminal illness or simply when they recognize that their decline is accelerating and that death is imminent, they need time to adjust to the realization, and denial is a mechanism that permits a longer time frame during which they can adjust more fully to such devastating ideas. It is quite common for people who are told they are going to die from some disease such as cancer to say such things as, "I am going to fight this thing and win" or "I want another opinion; I don't think you are right" or "I want to know who the leading doctors in this area are so I can get the best treatment." These are all denials; these people are terminally ill and have no chance of surviving, yet they persist in acting as if they will somehow overcome their condition.

A number of years ago, injections from some derivative of peach pits were touted as a cure for certain types of cancers. Since this drug was not approved for use in the United States, clinics were set up along the Mexican border where, for a substantial fee, patients could obtain the treatment. Americans flocked to these clinics in hope of being able to prove their doctors wrong. The less realistic believed that they would live; the more realistic figured that they had nothing to lose since they were going to die anyway. All these people were in a state of denial; they were attempting to overcome the reality of their impending deaths by finding any means that would offer them hope of not dying, no matter how farfetched.

For elderly parents who realize that they are dying, denial can be a comfort. Denial allows them to cling to hope and to pretend that they will be all right. Some people never get beyond this stage, or at least cling to it for as long as they are able. Denial does not simply go away, and, though it may fade, it can reemerge at a later time. Often, people mistake this stage for a phenomenon that must be challenged. Adult children may become embroiled in trying to prove to their elderly parents that they are in fact dying. Sometimes, of course, they do this for practical reasons, to get their parents to tie together loose ends. Often, however, such attempts are motivated by the adult children's own needs; if their parents accept the gravity of the situation, if they face up to death, they can begin to comfort their children about the loss to come. This is too much to ask! We adult children must put our own needs aside and tend to the viewpoint and needs of our dying parents. It is less important that the loose ends are tied together or that we feel comforted than that we strive to be where our dying parents are as they encounter the experience of dying. True, it is not easy to see beyond our own desires, or to drop practical realities and accept what our loved ones need at this difficult time, but it is an act of love to do so.

The second stage described by Kübler-Ross is that of *anger*. At some point, most dying individuals give up denial and begin to rage against their fate. They feel furious that death is happening to them. This feeling of being unfairly selected is common. The dying frequently see it as an injustice that they should be afflicted. They may ask, "Why me? Why now? I have been a good person; I have lived a moral existence. There are many people who deserve to die much more than I do. This is unfair!" Such thinking assumes that life is fair, which of course is not the case. Death occurs with no regard to who we are or what we have done. The anger people feel at this juncture is usually diffuse; it extends to virtually everything and everybody who is near them. They may call their children selfish, wicked, ungrateful, and so on. They may seem to be embittered about what otherwise are small considerations. They may complain incessantly about the quality of food or care or about how the view from their window is obscured, or they may be angry about the outcome of a baseball game, or that their room is too cold. Of course, the anger is not really intended for the target, but it is often difficult for adult children to keep this in perspective. It is easy to become frustrated with angry and unruly parents, and adult children may make matters worse by responding in kind. Or, just as futilely, adult children may run around apologizing to their parents, or for their parents' behavior. Worse yet, they may find themselves avoiding their parents altogether, finding excuses for not visiting them. None of these behaviors can help the situation. Your parent's rage must be understood, not exacerbated. It should not be taken at face value. It should not be taken personally. There is no need to apologize for it, as the professionals that care for your parent will understand it; indeed, they will expect it. Most importantly, you should not run away from it; abandoning your dying parent will increase his anxiety and rage, and intensify the guilt you experience after your parent dies.

It is important to recognize that your parent's anger is a normal, if difficult, response to dying. If you can do so, you can begin to understand this behavior rather than taking it personally and becoming embroiled in it more intensely. It is often helpful to process your reactions with another person, perhaps another family member or a professional. Find an appropriate setting to vent your feelings, especially your anger and frustration. If you seek the services of a minister or counselor, do not feel like you must be rational and calm. Feel free to let your feelings out; it is in your best interest and that of your dying parent to do so.

The next stage is called *bargaining*. In its most basic form, bargaining is an attempt to extend life by making a deal. Sometimes, bargains are made with God, such as when the dying individual promises to do some sort of penance to ward off deterioration and death. Sometimes, the bargain is with the doctor or a loved one. Almost everyone has encountered at least one story where an elderly person who is given only a short period of time to live miraculously struggles to make it to a birth, a wedding, or some other meaningful occasion, and then expires shortly afterwards. Usually, surviving family members take solace in the fact that this dying loved one made it to the event. In fact, when a dying person sets a goal like this, he is making a bargain to stave off the reality of death in a magical way. Almost universally, if the bargain is kept and the dying person does make it to the event, instead of dying fulfilled, he begins to formulate the next bargain.

Bargaining thus becomes a mechanism by which incremental steps are taken, each step being a small goal that seems magically reachable. Once the goal is met, a new bargain is made to take the next step. The overriding goal, of course, is to continue to live. Does a bargain actually extend life? In some instances, the bargain causes the person to focus more intensely upon living for a specific purpose, and this focus, sometimes referred to as a *will to live,* in rare instances may extend life in ways that are not fully understood. But this is not the rule; the ravages of time and disease must take their toll. However, bargaining often comforts dying people, as the bargain may give them an illusion that they can somehow have an impact on their hopeless situation. Bargaining often comforts family members as well, because it provides them with the illusion of a respite in the dying process. If Henrietta swears that she will live until her granddaughter is married, many family members breathe a sigh of relief and choose to believe her, even though her condition may be grave. The doctors do not give Henrietta long to live, but loved ones do not have to be concerned just yet; they can worry about the end later on. This illusion can be detrimental to those who buy into it. They can defer saying and doing things until it is too late, and this in turn can make their ultimate grief more intense and painful.

It is not uncommon to find healthy elderly people making bargains as well. I remember one vigorous octogenarian who regularly stated that he simply would not die until his great-grandchild was born. He made it to this date, so he then stated that he wanted to see her go to school. Next, he wanted to see her graduate from elementary school, an event he currently awaits. This man does not fall victim to the magical quality of bargaining, however, and put off such things as making a will. Thus, bargaining is beneficial to him; he sets limited future goals to strive for as his life progresses. In the same way, it is useful for adult children to recognize what this bargaining process is and to adjust to it from a realistic viewpoint. Do not defer important decisions or actions based on the words of aging or dying parents who are attempting to find a way to cling to life. Rather, realize that they need to do this now, but that you need to keep your own perspective grounded in reality, no matter how harsh it may be.

The next stage is *depression*. Of course, vast numbers of elderly parents experience forms of depression that are not related to their own dying. These sorts of depression are called *reactive,* that is, they arise out of reactions to events in their lives, both internal and external. Frequently, such depressions have to do with losses of loved ones. When friends die, the elderly experience both the loss and the realization that they may soon follow. Elderly people are constantly faced with the loss of personal function as well. A succession of such losses or a loss of great magnitude can result in significant depressive symptoms. There may be sadness and weeping, withdrawal and isolation, increased difficulty concentrating on tasks, memory impairment, appetite changes, sleep loss, slower reaction times, increased awareness of aches and pains, and even suicidal ideation – indeed, one of the largest groups of suicides is elderly men who live alone. In addition to reactive depression, the elderly often face depressions that we call *iatrogenic,* that is, caused by the complex interactions of various medications prescribed for them. I have seen many instances where drug interactions have been the direct cause of an elderly person's depression. If you suspect that your parent suffers from a depression of this type, or if you simply want to rule out the possibility, seek out a professional who specializes in the relatively new field of geriatric medicine. Specialists in this field know the various intricacies of prescribing medications for old people, and they can be consulted freely by you in conjunction with your parent's doctor.

Depression directly related to the dying process, however, is very different. Kübler-Ross describes such depression as *preparatory*. Preparatory depression occurs when dying people recognize that their death is impending and inevitable. At this point, they begin to realize that they will never again get to do things they used to do. There will never be another trip or another game of tennis. They will never go home again. They will never resume the life they once had. The finality of this realization is enormous; it is impossible to experience it and not become depressed.

Kübler-Ross describes how many people see loved ones in such a state of despair and respond by attempting to reassure them or to cheer them up. This is a mistake. Providing hope when there is none is not helpful. Reassurance that they may continue to live is false. Some dying people cling to this reassurance, which only pulls them away from the natural process of dying; others take such statements for what they are, an expression of their loved ones' need for hope, and respond by trying to comfort them – but it is they themselves who are dying and need the comfort!

What is useful at such a time? Support and nurturance and understanding. Allowing your dying parent to feel what he feels, letting him know that he is important and loved. Often, this can be accomplished without words, by means of holding his hand, stroking his brow, or giving him a kiss. Remember: *whatever your needs may be, your parent's needs are greater.* Your parent needs you to be there for him now, for the last time. Your needs can be dealt with elsewhere, at another time, because you will live to see another day. Your dying parent will not.

The final stage is *acceptance*. This stage is usually reached after passing through the others. Those who reach acceptance have established within themselves a sense of peace. They no longer feel the need to struggle for life and are no longer angry or depressed about their fate. While not content to die, they accept death. They are at a place where the demands of life are no longer central. They have given up the possibility of recovery and of holding on. They are more inwardly directed and often find external necessities like eating or medication or even visits burdensome and intrusive, for these interfere with their drifting toward death. Frequent periods of sleep and little communication are characteristic of this stage. Often, family members need more assistance at this point than the person who is dying, for the dying person accepts the end of life while family members feel the loss of their loved one acutely.

Remember that not all people go through all of these stages. Many die before reaching the stage of acceptance. Others cling desperately to denial, and some remain depressed. Your task is to know about these stages, to recognize them when they occur, and to attempt to help your loved one move along this continuum. The goal for all adult children should be to assist their parents in the natural process of dying and not to impede it. If your parent becomes stuck, perhaps you can help him free himself and move on. You may also try to enlighten other family members about what is going on. In this way, you can enlist their aid in helping your parent and perhaps avoid the various misunderstandings that often surround death. Of course, you yourself will have strong feelings and reactions to what is going on. Helping your parent die will not be easy for you; however, focusing on your needs is wrong. Your needs can be deferred or, if necessary, handled concurrently but separately from those of your dying parent. You must instead focus on the needs of your parent, for these are pressing.

Let us now turn to a story that shows how we can use some of these insights to understand what our parents experience as they go through the dying process.

Jenny was 76 when her doctor found suspicious hard masses in both of her breasts. Jenny herself had detected the lumps over two years earlier. She knew on one level that they could be malignant; she knew about the dangers of breast cancer and the need for early detection and treatment; she also knew that many die of this illness. And yet Jenny hesitated to obtain treatment. Why? The answer lies in her personal history.

Jenny was born in a large Midwestern city to an upper-middle-class family. Her father had been an accountant with his own firm. Her mother, though primarily a housewife, did quite well selling plaster statuettes of the Easter bunny, Santa Claus and his reindeer, and various other holiday subjects from her home. Jenny had two sisters and was close to them in childhood. One eventually moved away, but the other remained her best friend. After high school, Jenny worked for a while as a clerk in an insurance firm. Shortly thereafter, she met Rupert, fell in love, and was married. Jenny stopped working and began to raise a family.

Jenny and her husband had two sons and one daughter. The two sons were born during World War II. One was conceived before Rupert went into the service; the other was conceived when Rupert was home convalescing from a wound. The youngest child and only daughter, Randi, was born after the war. Rupert made a comfortable living working in advertising. Jenny was a dedicated "traditional" mother. She woke her children for school, prepared a family breakfast for her husband and children, kept up the house, prepared dinner, and was available to help her children with homework in the evenings.

In 1966, during the Vietnam War, Jenny's middle child was drafted into the army. Rupert encouraged him to fight for his country, but Jenny wanted him to remain home where he would be safe. In the end, Rupert's influence prevailed, and their son went into the service, even though he could have avoided the draft by getting a critical skills deferment. About 14 months after he joined the military, the son was reported missing in action. His body was never found.

This loss had a profound impact on Jenny. She blamed Rupert for their son's death. As a result, their relationship foundered. Before, Rupert had been a major source of leadership and decision-making in the family; now, Jenny treated him with contempt. The energy she had once put into the relationship now shifted away from Rupert. Since her other son had moved across the country and had little contact with his parents, Jenny sought solace and support from her daughter and her sister. Jenny and Randi had always been close; Jenny now clung to Randi, and Randi reciprocated. When Randi married, she moved only a few miles from her mother, and they saw each other almost daily. Jenny's sister lived a short walk from Jenny, and they, too, were constant companions.

Jenny's estrangement with Rupert continued. When he died of a heart attack in 1978, Jenny grieved, but there was a good deal of relief in being rid of the tension that had existed between them. Rupert's death brought Jenny and Randi even closer.

In 1989, Jenny's sister was diagnosed with late stage breast cancer. For the next 15 months, Jenny spent every day with her ailing sister, taking her to doctors, helping her through a mastectomy, supporting her through difficult treatments and chemotherapy. Her sister wanted to live and did everything she could to hold on to life. In the end, however, the cancer won, and Jenny watched her beloved sister waste away and die.

Jenny was heartbroken. In her grief, she became even closer to her daughter. Gradually, however, her sorrow abated, and she began to reestablish her life.

In 1992, about two years after her sister's death, Jenny discovered lumps in her own breasts. The loss of her sister should have taught Jenny that she needed immediate medical intervention. However, she did not seek it. Her initial response was one of disbelief, of *denial*. She told herself that this could not be happening to her, that God would not let it happen to the same family twice, even though it was highly likely that she had the same illness as her sister. She convinced herself that she felt fine and that the lumps were nothing to worry about. It was some time before Jenny told her daughter about the lumps. When she finally did, Randi implored her mother to go to a physician, but in vain.

Emotionally, Jenny could not deal with the idea that she could have cancer. She had residual feelings of loss from the death of her son, from the failure of her marriage, from her other son's noninvolvement, and from Rupert's death. In addition, she was not fully recovered from her sister's prolonged and agonizing death. How could she face more losses, how could she go through the process of cancer diagnosis and treatment, a process that had been so painful for her to watch such a short time before? To her mind, cancer was simply unacceptable, so she denied the potential reality and refused to see a physician. She minimized the symptoms and held fast to the irrational belief that the same disease would never strike the same family twice. Randi continued to implore her mother, so Jenny eventually gave in, not because she was ready to face the problem, but because she saw her daughter's anxiety. When her doctor expressed his concern and set up an immediate visit to a cancer specialist, Jenny still resisted. She told the doctor that she was sure he was overreacting. At Randi's insistence, however, Jenny went to the specialist, who confirmed the diagnosis of late stage cancer. He recommended the same course of treatment her sister had undergone.

Jenny could no longer deny the reality. She faced the fact that she had a life-threatening cancer, and this made her extremely *angry*. Her anger took the form of rage at her doctors. She ranted about how these "high and mighty" physicians thought they were so powerful and omnipotent and godlike – yet, for all of their pretensions, they could not save her sister. Now, they wanted to make her suffer the way her sister had.

Jenny was furious that she had cancer. Nevertheless, she made the decision to forgo treatment. In some instances, this is a rational and humane decision; the sufferer opts for a shorter but quality life instead of a painful and uncertain treatment. But Jenny's decision to forgo treatment seems to have been influenced by her intense anger at dying, which she directed at her doctors for not saving her sister and for putting her sister through procedures that made her suffer. This displaced anger made her want to pay back those doctors, and she did so by presenting herself as a victim who would not allow her doctors even to attempt to save her. She was hostile on her visits, saying such things as, "With all of your money and education, you can't even help one old woman!" When the doctors repeated how they wanted to help her, Jenny would remind them how ineffectual they had been in helping her sister. "Why should I be another guinea pig?"

Eventually, as Jenny's condition worsened, she required brief hospitalizations and more care at home. Randi provided this care tirelessly. She even moved into Jenny's home, so she could be available all the time. Randi's devotion to her mother took a great toll on her. As Jenny saw her daughter become more fatigued and tired out, she entered the stage of *bargaining*. Jenny worried what would happen to her daughter after she died. Since Randi had been divorced and had no children, and her brother was far away, she would be all alone. Jenny feared that her connection to her daughter was all that kept Randi going. Without Jenny, what would Randi have in life? Thus, Jenny *bargained* for time. She asked God to let her live until Christmas. Later, she asked to live until her birthday, and then to Randi's birthday. In effect, she attempted to keep herself going, hoping to remain her daughter's companion until her daughter no longer needed her. This thinking was not rational. The fact that Randi spent so much time caring for Jenny precluded her finding any meaningful relationships. Furthermore, Randi was a competent adult who was capable of being responsible for her own life and did not need her mother. Jenny's bargain was dictated by her predicament and her distorted perception of it.

If Jenny had lived a while longer, she might have reached the stage of depression and prepared herself for her impending death. Acceptance may have even been achieved. However, Jenny did not live long enough to progress to these stages.

It was not the cancer that killed her in the end. Jenny was still living in her apartment, with medications to control her pain. On days when she felt strong enough, she would have Randi take her across the street where there was a bench next to a park. There she could sit in the fresh air and feel part of the world. One day, after Randi had gone inside to make a quick phone call, Jenny got up from the bench and walked between two parked cars into the street, where she was run over and killed. It was never clear why Jenny had ventured forth into the street. It could have been that she was chilled and wanted to come inside, or perhaps she experienced some confusion and error in judgment because of her medications. Randi believed that her mother had intended to die, that she had thrown herself in front of the car in order to put an end to her suffering. Earlier that day, her mother had stated that she wished God would take her and that she just could not tolerate her pain any longer. Oddly, just before Randi went to make the phone call, Jenny had also made a point of telling Randi how much she loved her and how much she appreciated her sacrifices. In retrospect, Randi believes this was her mother's way of saying good-bye. After her mother's death, Randi sought professional counseling in order to deal with the effects of this painful period, and she was able to work out her issues and go on with her life.

In Jenny's example, we see the power of Kübler-Ross's formulation of the dying process. But Kübler-Ross's framework can be employed in another manner. We can apply her steps not only to the dying, but also to the people who are caring for an aging or dying loved one. Applied in this way, Kübler-Ross's steps can help us understand both the first good-bye and the second good-bye.

In earlier chapters, we have seen how we adult children frequently fail to recognize when our formerly strong, independent parents need additional care. We may miss the fact that our aged parents are not caring for themselves adequately or need assistance with simple tasks. This is *denial* of the reality of our aged parents' new status in life. We do not want to give up the illusion that our parents are still there for us as they always have been, that we can still rely on them to provide us with unconditional positive regard and support, for such a recognition involves a massive and possibly painful psychological shift. It is important to be aware of this denial and to overcome it. Otherwise, we miss the reality of our aged parents' situation and neglect their need for us to take a more active role in their lives. Some of us never get out of this stage. We fail to respond to our parents' needs because we cannot see beyond our own. However, once we realize intellectually that such a stage exists, it becomes possible to dialogue with friends and loved ones to assess whether or not we are in denial and, if we are, to do something about it.

Once denial is passed through, we adult children may find ourselves in an *angry* mood much of the time. This may take the form of short-temperedness towards our aged parents, a common expression of such anger. We may argue with them a lot, sometimes violently, or find ourselves overly irritated by their incapacities or quirks. Sometimes, our anger takes the form of not communicating with them as often as we should or not inviting them to family functions. The issues that seem to be bothering us are not central to this response. Rather, they are convenient mechanisms for having an internal and immature rage at the change in roles that is taking place. In reality, we are expressing the anger that we feel towards our aged parents for no longer being our support system, for making us be their support. Our parents, on whom we depended physically and emotionally, are now making ever-increasing demands on us, and we resent it. Objectively, of course, it is harder now to deal with them; they are cranky or they tire easily, or they cannot eat a lot of foods, and so on. Have we really become intolerant of the people who raised us and nurtured us? No. Tolerance is not the issue. On a deeper level, it is our own anger at the change in roles that moves us, and we displace this anger when we overreact to relatively inconsequential events. If we can be introspective enough to look at our own behavior and recognize it as a stage, it becomes possible to make other and more productive choices about how to act.

Our experience of the stage of *bargaining* can take a variety of forms. Bargaining is a way of quasi-magically "making a deal" to ensure that things work out happily, and many of us bargain in this sense as a mechanism for assuring that our parents will continue to be there for us, or that the the aging process will bring on no further dysfunction. We may believe that if we state the bargain out loud, as if it were an incantation, things will magically turn out the way we hope. "Just let him not have Alzheimer's" and "Please let her behave appropriately at this event" are examples of bargaining in this sense. But bargains do not change reality. We must learn to accept the facts, and we must formulate plans to deal with them realistically. We must all be aware that a tendency to magical thinking is a likely factor in our relations with our aging parents, and make sure that it does not hamper our effectiveness in dealing with their problems.

We experience the stage of *depression* in the same way our dying parents do, as a preparation for their eventual death. When adult children are faced with grave circumstances, such as their parents' hospitalization for a terminal condition, depression is common and understandable. But even significantly earlier, when our parents are functional but declining, depression is common. Symptoms of depression coincide with our aware-ness that our beloved parents are slipping away from us. Depression also emanates from the recognition that we assume their place in the chain of life after they are gone. We become aware of our own decline, and this requires a period of adjustment during which depression is a possible experience. If we acknowledge such a stage, we can seek the support we need to come through it successfully. We need to discuss our fears and to have them responded to by those who love us or by professionals who understand our point of view.

Finally, there is *acceptance,* acceptance of our aged parents' demise, whether it comes on slowly as part of the process of increasing dysfunc-tion or suddenly or rapidly as a result of trauma or terminal disease. There is also acceptance of the reality that they are no longer there for us as they once were, and there is acceptance of the inevitability that we will assume their place as the aging parents of our own adult children.

Let us see how this five-stage framework can apply to some actual experiences of adult children coping with the aging and death of their parents.

Matt was at work when he got the call that his 81-year-old father had been rushed to the hospital after a household accident. Matt was 40 years old and worked as the manager of a supermarket. He lived in the neighborhood where he had grown up, just a few blocks from his father's apartment. Matt was an only child who had been very close with his father. They had played ball together when he was a boy, and his father still came to watch Matt's company softball games. In fact, his father was at the game two nights before, cheering and congratulating Matt when he made a hit that scored two runs. Matt had spoken to his father on the phone the night before the accident, and they had made plans to go out to dinner after Matt's game that very evening.

When he got the call, Matt could not believe it, and at first he minimized the event. He told his staff that his father had been taken to the hospital and that he needed to get over there to see what was happening. At the hospital, he was told that his father was in surgery. Apparently, the old man had climbed up on a chair to reach some dishes on the top shelf of a cupboard and had fallen off, hitting his head on the floor. A neighbor had heard the crash and called 911. Matt was told that there was internal hemorrhaging and that the situation was serious. Matt remembers thinking that his dad was tough and would be just fine. He did not believe that anything serious could happen. After all, his dad had survived the War and the Depression and his mother's death, and he would get through this. Matt understood the facts intellectually, but he failed to synthesize them. He was in a state of *denial,* trying not to deal with the gravity of the situation by pretending that it was not really that bad. The doctors told Matt that his father's fall had been caused by a stroke and that massive bleeding had damaged the brain stem; surgery had not relieved the pressure in time and significant brain damage had occurred. Still, Matt continued to deny the gravity of the situation. When he was finally able to sit at his father's bedside, Matt felt certain that his dad would open his eyes at any minute and begin to speak.

Finally, the doctors informed Matt that his father was brain dead and would not recover, that only the life support equipment was keeping his body alive. Matt's father was, in effect, already gone. It took Matt a while to grasp this fact. Once he did, he immediately became *angry.* He raged at his father for being so stupid as to climb on a chair at his age, he raged at himself for not having been there, and he bitterly criticized the doctors for not having saved his father. He was even infuriated by the incessant noise of the life support equipment.

Matt was advised that it was now his decision whether or not to turn off the life support machines and let his father die naturally. He was told that it was not clear how long death would take. Matt found himself delaying this decision, and he began to formulate a *bargain*. He knew that if the equipment were turned off, his dad would surely die; but he told himself that if he delayed, maybe a miracle would happen. Perhaps his father would open his eyes for just a minute, and he could possibly have one last hug, one last kiss, one last exchange of words. Finally, as the hours passed, Matt reached a point where he stopped holding on to his hopes and began to *prepare* for his father's death. He released his deep sadness by weeping. He had flashbacks of many of the good times he had shared with his father. Finally, Matt was ready to let his father go. He *accepted* the fact that his father was brain dead and that soon his body would die, too. The life support was disconnected. Matt held his father's hand as he died.

Now, Matt had to deal with his grief and guilt over his father's death. It was during this period, after the funeral, after the friends and neighbors were tired of hearing Matt talk about his father, that Matt sought counseling to help him resolve his loss. It took some time, but he finally adjusted to his father's absence from his life.

Matt's story illustrates how Kübler-Ross's stages can be seen operating in adult children as they lose their parents. Understanding the reactions that we are likely to have as our parents age and die can make the emotional difficulties we face during this period easier to manage. Most importantly, if we can understand and manage our own difficulties, we free ourselves to focus on and respond to the needs of our elderly parents.

Matt's story involved the sudden death of a parent who had been functioning independently. Let us now turn to a story that will show how Kübler-Ross's stages apply to an adult child whose parent declines slowly and gradually.

Tom had always been disappointed that his father, Walter, was not someone he could admire. Through education and hard work, Tom had become a successful and affluent banker, but his father had barely made it through high school. Walter lacked the sophistication that Tom had acquired and, therefore, did not fit into Tom's social circle. In fact, Tom made sure to keep his relationship with his father completely separate. Tom had always resented the fact that his friends at college and graduate school had fathers who supported and guided them, while he had only a limited and uneducated father who could do neither of these things. Unfortunately, Tom could not see that Walter had done his best, that he had sacrificed for his son and had tried to help him in whatever way he could. In fact, Walter had succeeded in giving Tom opportunities that far exceeded those available to his friends in the old neighborhood. Tom's reference point, however, was no longer the old neighborhood, but rather the world of his current peer group, a world composed of successful clients and colleagues. In this world, despite his achievements, Tom still felt inadequate and insecure; in his heart, he did not feel that he belonged there, but he projected those feelings onto his father and criticized him instead.

Tom's contact with his father was almost inconsequential. There were short, often terse, weekly phone calls. There were obligatory visits, generally arranged around another event so that the contact was minimal. As time progressed, Walter, who lived alone, began to lose his ability to function. Gradually, it became more difficult for him to attend to various tasks, such as shopping and maintaining the house. Tom noticed that things remained undone, that the lawn was not neatly trimmed, the door needed oiling, and the eves needed to be cleaned out, but he refused to acknowledge that his father needed more help from him. Instead, he would tell himself that his father just had not gotten around to doing the work, or he simply added "lazy" or "unkempt" to his list of grievances. Tom did not want to see that Walter needed his help. Tom remained in *denial* for a long time.

One day, Walter sprained his ankle badly. Now, Tom could not deny his father's need, so he began to help with the chores. However, he told himself that this was merely a temporary situation, that his help would only be needed until Walter was back on his feet. Since Tom had to spend more time at his father's house, he began to hear from the neighbors how good it was that Tom was helping out. Apparently, Walter had needed help for a long time, but had been too proud to ask for it. As the neighbors continued to express their expectation that Tom's help would be permanent, Tom came to realize that Walter was no longer able to function on his own. However, the prospect of taking responsibility for his father on a long-term basis made Tom *angry*. He asked himself why he should be stuck having to guide and support his father, when his father had never guided or supported him. He became quite irritable and short-tempered. He was often sarcastic with Walter and complained about the tasks he had to do for him. Walter bore his son's behavior in silence. He was aware that he needed Tom, and he could not risk a breach that might cut him off from Tom's help. And so life went on, rather uncomfortably for both.

The confrontation between father and son came a few years later, after Walter moved into an older adult complex. At this facility, Walter had a whole new set of supports. Since Tom was no longer saddled with his father's chores, he dropped his visits down to the minimum. One day, Walter blew up at him. He accused Tom of being a condescending, pompous social climber who had forgotten his roots and shirked his obligations. He expressed his disappointment that his son pursued material success at the expense of common decency.

I would like to report that this confrontation led to some positive growth and to an eventual reconciliation. Unfortunately, however, it resulted in contact that was less frequent and even more strained. My knowledge of this situation is based on observations and discussions with Tom, Walter, and our neighbors. I grew up with Tom, and I am still in contact with him as an old acquaintance. Walter is now in a nursing home, and Tom still visits him out of obligation and continues to resent these visits. Tom has often said that he wishes his father would not be so hostile and just accept Tom's material success.

Clearly, Tom does not understand his own behavior in the changed circumstances brought on by his father's decline. Tom is stuck at the stage of anger. He occasionally bargains, as when he mentions that perhaps his father will live long enough to mellow out a bit, and then they can get along better. Obviously, there are indications of guilt and depression to come. But Tom has not accepted who his father is now or that his father needs his help.

We must handle ourselves better than Tom did when our own aged parents decline, become increasingly dependent upon us, and eventually die. The stages posited by Kübler-Ross can guide us through this painful process. Let them help you deepen your self-awareness as well as your understanding and compassion for your elderly parents. Let them help you put structure around experiences that otherwise remain amorphous. If you do so, you will be able to tend to your parents' needs with greater tolerance, insight, understanding, sensitivity, and competence.

The call came through at about 10:30 p.m. My sister-in-law informed me that my mother had been rushed to the hospital. She was being examined by the doctors, and we would have more details later on. I was stunned. Could this be my mother's last night of life? A few moments before, I had been walking on my treadmill, working off the stresses of the day and watching television. Now, suddenly, I was faced with what I had always known would happen, at least intellectually. I thought I had prepared myself for this eventuality. Certainly, I had spent a lot of time thinking and reading and talking about it. In that moment, however, I knew that emotionally I was not prepared at all. I had done many of the right things, but no actions or rehearsals could prepare me for this situation. I was afraid and nervous. I was sad and angry. I was guilty and worried. Above all, I was confused. I wanted to believe that the doctors would discover that my mother was not really as bad off as they had initially thought, that she might even turn out to be fine or only partially affected. I tried to convince myself that my mother would live. I worked hard to deny the reality of her impending death.

At midnight, the phone rang again. This time, my sister-in-law told me that my mother was brain dead and that I should meet my brothers and father at the hospital the next day so that together we could make the decision to turn off her life support. When I hung up, I had a terrible sinking feeling in the pit of my stomach. How could this be? I could not accept it. Nevertheless, I busied myself with tasks – plane reservations, packing, canceling patient appointments, all the mundane details that I had to take care of before I could go to New York. Part of me welcomed this as a means of pushing my feelings aside. Yet each task reminded me of its ultimate purpose. I needed emergency reservations for the airlines, so I had to explain myself, and I broke down as I did so. As I packed, I had to remind myself to take a black suit for the funeral. My partner had to be told what was happening, so she could inform my patients. On the plane, I cried intermittently. People tried not to intrude, but I am sure many wondered what was happening. When I got to New York, I hailed a taxi. I told the driver to get me to the hospital quickly. I am not sure what possessed me, but I kept pushing the driver. "Can't you go any faster?" "Why is this taking so long?" "Come on, move it." At times, I was shouting at the poor fellow. Inside, I had this terrible need to be with my mother, and I could not wait a second longer.

When I arrived, I went right up to her room. There she was, hooked up to the machines that kept her alive. She looked like my mother, only asleep. I leaned over and kissed her and almost expected that she would open her eyes and say, "Hi, Davey, I'm glad you are here." She could not, of course. Oh, how I wished she could! Here was someone I loved, that I would do anything for, and yet I could do nothing to help her. I felt helpless and useless. When I met up with the other family members, they told me that, ironically, paramedics had been passing by the apartment building when my mother was stricken; their quick action saved her body, but nothing could save her mind. We all gathered together and wept and talked about what to do. The doctors made it clear that there was no hope – her mind had been destroyed. Only the life support machines kept her body alive. Lying there, she still looked like my mother, but her personality and her loving, gentle nature were gone!

I can remember wishing desperately for one more chance to hear her call my name – she was the only one who called me "Davey" and I so wanted to hear her say it. What I would have given to have one more hug and kiss! And yet I knew this could never be.

We all decided to have the life support removed and to let her body catch up with her mind. After some legalities, the doctor removed the equipment and left us alone. My father stood next to her and kissed her. My older brother held her hand. My sister-in-law stood at the foot of the bed. I held her other hand. My younger brother stood with his hands in his pockets, surveying the room from the doorway. We were all silent.

It was, perhaps, the most difficult thing I have done in my life – standing there, looking upon my mother for the last time, holding her hand and feeling the pulse slow down and then stop. It took about 40 minutes, they told me later. Time seemed suspended for me. I felt calm, sad, numb, and in pain, all at once. The whole experience had an unreal quality. She looked as if she could sit up at any moment, yet I knew this was the last time I would ever be able to touch her, or see her, or be near her. Watching her die was a very painful thing for all of us, but we all recognized that it was a task we could not avoid. She deserved to have her family with her as she finally relinquished life. She had given all of us so much love and understanding while she was alive; we owed it to her to be there when she died. So there we were, gathered around her, all silent, to be with her to the last. It was a peaceful, loving moment that we shared with her. We all encountered our sense of loss, but we also touched her and loved her and were with her as she died.

Afterwards, I felt bewildered. It was hard to make any sense out of this experience. I think I was numbed by the intensity of it. As my keyed-up emotions calmed, I was overtaken by fatigue. I stayed with my father, and we tried to console each other. We both felt an empty hole in our lives. Mercifully, the strain of the day eventually caught up with us, and we both fell into a deep sleep.

The funeral brought back memories of her death. Many friends and family were supportive and loving. They could not make up for the pain. I felt as if I were operating on automatic pilot much of the time. I stayed with my father through the period of his mourning. During that time, I had to help my octogenarian father adjust to life without the companion he had lived with for 55 years. I had to teach him how to do some basic tasks, like cooking simple meals and washing clothes. The more difficult adjustment of suddenly living without her, of getting into bed only to find there is no one else there, I had to leave to him alone.

I still miss my mother. Several years have passed since her death, but she is still often in my thoughts. Losing her is no longer a central theme in my life, as it was for the first year. I no longer call home and forget she is not there. I no longer think I see her on the street. Now, I remember her on Mother's Day, on her birthday, on the anniversary of her death. Sometimes, I see a book or trinket in a store that I think my mother would have liked or some garment that is just her style. The other night, I caught a movie on cable that brought back memories of seeing the same film in a theater with my mother many years ago. I remembered how much she had laughed — until her face was covered with tears. I could, for an instant, hear her laughter and feel the closeness that we shared. I missed her in that moment, but I also knew how lucky I was to have had such a person in my life.

CHAPTER SIX

OUR JOURNEY CONTINUES

Some of the observations I have offered to you have been based on my academic training, some on research, still others on my own clinical practice. Woven throughout these chapters are observations based on my own experience with my mother's slow decline and eventual death, as well as on my father's responsive and patient attitude. My point of view throughout this book has been greatly influenced by what I have gone through with my mother and am currently facing with my father. In short, I want you to know that I am a person like you, who has faced many of the situations described in this book. I know what it is like to deal with an aging parent's life, not only because I am a professional, but because I am a son. I know what it feels like to see parents you love decline and gradually lose more and more of the uniqueness that made them who they were. I have felt the helplessness of watching this process unfold and being unable to halt it. I have encountered the realization that I will soon be the aged parent facing issues around my own mortality.

People whose experiences with elderly parents are different from mine may find some of my observations at odds with what they have come to know. Such differences are useful because they encourage readers to focus on and define their own positions. However, my professional as well as my personal experience has taught me that we are more alike than we are different. None of us can do much about the fact that our parents will age, decline, and eventually die, and none of us can change the fact that we, too, will age and take their place as aged parents. What we can do a great deal about is how we as adult children behave as we go through this difficult time, and here we all have the same goals: to be sensitive, caring, communicative, and realistic partners to our aged parents; to act as a resource that is reliable, consistent, and supportive.

We must not be indifferent or unresponsive to our aging parents, and we must not allow our own fears to lead us into denying their ever-increasing deficiencies. True, some adult children do retreat into indifference and denial; but perhaps the stories and observations in this book can help such people to renew their commitment as sons and daughters and to find a more realistic and more helpful approach. After all, many of our negative responses are, in fact, simply ways of protecting ourselves from the ambiguity of the situation and from the difficulty of dealing with our own confused feelings. Those of us who feel negative emotions, who are lost or confused about how to respond and what to do, should be aware that it is normal to feel ambivalent at this time. In fact, it is the act of stifling such emotions, of holding them inside and not sharing them, that magnifies and intensifies them and makes them unhealthy. If we are to manage this painful period successfully, we must acknowledge that we feel the way we do and then begin to release and deal with our feelings. We must not remain paralyzed and inert. Instead, we must strive to understand and resolve what inhibits us. We must examine our deepest conflicts and motivations and see how these influence our judgment, our attitude, and our behavior. Working on ourselves in this way can be painful and laborious, but it is also immensely rewarding. We free ourselves to live happier and more productive lives, and, more to the point, we achieve the understanding that allows us to become better adult children.

Working on ourselves frees us to relate to our aged parents in a more meaningful way. It enables us to begin to comprehend their viewpoint and to understand how their viewpoint affects their behavior. Knowing who we are and how we behave helps us to see, by contrast, who our parents are and how they behave. We can begin to observe how their complex pattern of behaviors and feelings resembles and diverges from our own. Above all, we must remember that it is our responsibility to act on our aged parents' behalf, no matter how we happen to feel. If we do not act for them, who will?

Advice such as this would have helped me greatly in dealing with my own mother's decline. I certainly muddled my way through that experience. I always found myself shocked by the progression of the various diseases from which she suffered. Whenever I prepared ahead to meet my mother's condition, I usually found that I had prepared for a previous, less advanced level of deterioration. No doubt denial played a role in this. My own need for nurturance would not allow me to let her go, and thus reduced my effectiveness in nurturing her. I see this now, and began to see it even then, but I still feel guilt about my failure to put her needs always above my own.

I recall an incident that illustrates the way in which my mother's ability to function was compromised by the progression of Alzheimer's disease. My mother always enjoyed watching television. She found it relaxing and entertaining. As I grew up, many evening hours found us on the couch in the living room watching our favorite shows together. We would talk often as we watched; we would laugh, perhaps have a snack. These were close, enjoyable times. In my adult years when I visited her, we watched television together whenever I was available. We both looked forward to it because it was and had been a time of closeness. I know how media critics are always negatively depicting television as a mechanism that impedes communication, but for us it was just the opposite – we talked and had a good and close time.

One semi-tradition we had was to watch the film *The Ten Commandments,* which was shown every year during my spring visit. This film had special meaning for us, not because of the content, but because of the memories associated with it. We had seen it when it first came out. It was playing at a large movie theater on Broadway in Manhattan. I was 10 years old at the time. My mother had gotten tickets for us and some friends. We all went down on the subway together, dressed nicely and very excited. I sat next to my mother while we watched this truly thrilling film. I remember that we bought some candy bars and ice cream "Bon Bons" at intermission. During the second half, my mother become so engrossed in the movie that she dropped a Bon Bon. It rolled down into her shoe and made her foot cold before she realized she had dropped it. We had a wonderful day, and the movie became special to both of us. Years later, whenever we watched the movie on television, she would laugh out loud while recalling how long it had taken her to realize that the Bon Bon was in her shoe. The incident had been funny at the time, and now it always brought a smile, not so much for the humor, but because it connected us to a special memory about a close experience.

About 14 months before she died, my mother and I watched the movie yet again. It was the same pleasant experience it had always been: familiar and relaxed and close. One year later, we did it again, but this time things were very different. The previous year, she had displayed only minimal symptoms of Alzheimer's disease; this time, she was a good deal worse. She must have asked me 10 separate times what we were going to watch. Within a few minutes, she would forget my answer. During the film, she constantly asked me what was going on. She wondered again and again what the name of the film was, who the actors were, and what was happening. Here was a film she had seen so many times that she could practically recite every line, and she could not understand the simplest aspects of it – she could not even remember the title! This brought home to me how much she had deteriorated. I was greatly saddened to see how difficult it was for her to deal with even something so familiar. At the same time, I was utterly distraught because something so precious to both of us had been taken away. Intellectually, I had anticipated some deterioration in her, but my emotional attachment to her had led me to underestimate it. As a result, I was shocked and upset, and therefore less able to be there for her.

I remember another time when I was shocked at my mother's deterioration. When my mother attended the Bar Mitzvah of my son, she was fine; two years later, when she attended the Bat Mitzvah of my daughter, she was disoriented and confused. The ceremonies themselves and the subsequent celebrations were very much alike. The plane trip my parents took was the same, and their participation in the event was very similar. With so much alike, it was quite striking how different my mother had become in those two years. During the ceremony, various members of the family and close friends were honored by standing before the congregation and saying a particular Hebrew prayer. My mother and father were to come up and recite this prayer. Before the first ceremony, my mother quite lucidly asked me to help her prepare for her portion because she had not done such a thing in many decades. I reassured her and explained exactly how it would work and that someone would be there to assist her. All of her concern was for naught, because she and my father went up and did their parts flawlessly, my mother performing especially well. She also thoroughly enjoyed herself at the party afterwards. But how different she was two years later at the Bat Mitzvah for my daughter! Alzheimer's disease had taken its toll. My mother was still the sweet individual she had always been, and she looked outwardly the same. Her mental ability, however, had deteriorated dramatically. She was often confused. When I picked her up at the airport, she knew who I was, but she was not sure where she was or why she had come, and I had to tell her several times. Throughout the weekend, she became disoriented frequently. Obviously, it was difficult for her to be away from her own home and familiar surroundings. On several occasions, she called me by my older brother's name and thought my son and daughter were his children. She repeated herself constantly; she must have related an incident about the food on the plane 20 times. Each time, I responded as if I had never heard the story before rather than distress her by making her aware of her repetition. At the ceremony, she stood up at several points and asked me in a loud voice, "Davey, am I in the right spot?" Each time she did so, I patiently reassured her that she was fine. Because such ceremonies are family-oriented and relatively relaxed, no one in the congregation took offense, and things went along quite expeditiously. At the social gathering afterwards, many people, recognizing my mother's limitations, patiently and sensitively spent time with her. I tried to be near her often, but my responsibility as a host kept pulling me away. Her behavior was much the same, repeating herself constantly, not sure where she was or why she was there. My mother, though, was enormously good-natured. She did not comprehend why she was at this party, but she nonetheless recognized it as a social event and made every effort to go with the flow. At the airport on the way home, my mother became confused and upset when something in her pockets set off the metal detector. The airport personnel soon realized her state of mind, and we were able to proceed to the plane. Throughout this visit, I did my best to respond to my mother in a patient and caring way. Inside, however, I was shocked and disturbed to see the sharp contrast between her condition now and her condition just two years before. Still, I could take comfort in the fact that, although my mother's mind was not the same, her sweet disposition remained, and her disposition aided her in dealing with her confusion. As difficult as it was for me to confront my mother's shortcomings, it must have been infinitely more difficult for her. Four days after she left on the plane, she had the stroke which ultimately led to her death.

I was pained and saddened to see my mother so drastically affected by Alzheimer's disease within two short years. At quiet moments, when I had the luxury of solitude and I thought about her deterioration, I felt tears running down my cheeks. It took an enormous effort to deal with my grief and then to pull out of it and focus upon her needs – an effort I did not always succeed in making. Repressing my feelings would have made matters worse; I had to acknowledge them and cope with them. I knew that if I used my energy to hold back my emotions, I might not be as available as I should to assist my mother. She needed me to be open and sensitive to her anxieties about the realities we must face together.

I urge you to learn from my efforts and my mistakes. Do not allow your difficulty accepting the loss of your parent keep you from being responsive to that parent when he or she needs you the most. I urge you to understand your own feelings and to deal with them, to fight denial, to comprehend your aged parent's point of view, and to balance this view against the facts in which you are both embedded. Do not allow yourself to miss important information that, if synthesized properly, could enhance the quality of your parent's life and, perhaps, even end up saving it. These are not inconsequential issues.

There is generational continuity in this process of saying good-bye to our parents. They said good-bye to their parents, and one day our children will say good-bye to us. We witnessed how our parents responded to the needs of their own parents; we watched and perhaps have emulated behaviors that we may, upon reflection, now consider more or less appropriate to our own individual situations. Likewise, our children will observe and perhaps emulate the way we respond to our aged parents now. Our parents assumed the position of their parents as the aging patriarch and matriarch of the family. Now we our moving toward that position. For many of us, years have passed when we never really considered our parents' role or our own role in the cycle of life. Every so often, however, changes occurred that would remind us. Now that the aging process is clearly taking its toll on our parents, we are forced to confront the reality that roles inevitably change over time. As our parents become more dependent, we must become more responsible. As our parents age, so do we; as our parents move closer toward death, so do we.

For many, this brush with mortality is reason enough to turn away from the fact that our parents need us. As we have seen, such behavior, no matter how human, can lead to great suffering for our aged parents and for us. We pay a significant price for acting in this manner, for we cut ourselves off from one of the sources of our humanity. Ideally, recognizing our parents' mortality should lead us to become more aware, not less aware, of our own position in the evolution and continuity of life. First, we must give up our childhood image of the strong, life-giving, protective, and nurturing parents who were responsible for our safety and well-being. Next, we must accept the reality that our parents need our help as we once needed theirs, and we must take action to help them as they once helped us. Finally, we must carry out our duty of teaching our own children about the responsibilities they may one day assume when we ourselves approach death. This is the unbroken chain, the continuity in our lives, and it bears in no small part on our dignity as human beings.

To become the caretaker of those who once took care of us is not an easy thing. It involves a change both externally and internally. Externally, our behavior must now be directed to identifying and responding to a progressive series of changes that our aged parents are going through. These include changes in health, attitude, lifestyle, mood, and level of functioning, just to name a few. Internally, we as adult children must reorient ourselves: we must become our parents' parents, and we must bring our perception of our aged parents into line with their altered reality. They no longer are the people who cared for us; they are now people we must care for. The illusion that most of us maintain, that somehow our parents will always be available to help us in time of trouble – help that most adults do not actually require, but remain emotionally attached to – must give way to the realization that our parents can no longer be our caretakers, that we must now be theirs. This is not an easy leap to make, for in order to make it we must redefine ourselves. We must shed our old emotional connection to dependency; we must acknowledge our independence and autonomy; and we must shoulder new responsibilities.

In the course of this book, we have met a variety of people, both adult children and aged parents. I have tried to provide the reader with an understanding of both points of view and of how these views interact with one another. Some of the people in these stories have not been particularly successful, while others are in progress, moving toward a desired outcome. All such relations are, of course, highly complex. While specific personalities vary and a host of circumstantial variables exist, the overall experience is, to a large extent, universal in nature and human in scope. Most of us will struggle with our shift in role as we watch our parents age, need us ever-increasingly, and eventually die. But most of us will do the best we can to face and live up to our responsibilities, for this is the continuity of our existence. We may find it disconcerting that life progresses to its end, but we may also derive an inner strength from the idea that the chain of existence passes on to those who are next in line, our children. In a sense, this makes us immortal, not in an individualistic way, but in a larger sense: humanity goes on and we are part of that collectivity. There is a certain reassurance in this concept, this idea that we may not go on as who we are, but we will go on as contributors, both genetically and humanly, to the destiny and dignity of our kind.

Intellectually, I had been aware that, of course, this frail woman who had heart disease and Alzheimer's, and who did not have the wherewithal to take care of herself, would eventually die. On an emotional level, however, I was taken by surprise. Even though I was a mental health professional who had read about death and had counseled numerous people through the grieving process, I had no idea of the impact that my mother's death would have upon me. It was not just the immediate shock and the almost surreal events that surrounded her death. These were, of course, quite terrible, as I have described before. Rather, it was the sense of emptiness that seemed to be constantly with me after she was gone. Nothing felt right. For some time, I felt as if I were going through the motions of life devoid of the substance. This person, this anchor, who always afforded me an unconditional love and positive regard no matter what the circumstances, was suddenly gone from my life, and I was left to manage without her. It is not as if I did not have the skills to carry on. Certainly, I had managed my life competently for decades. And it was not as if I had seen her or spoken to her all that frequently in the years before her death; I called her once a week and, because of the distance between us, we visited perhaps three times a year. No, it was not the loss of those sustaining contacts, intermittent as they were, that impacted me — it was the fact that a psychological safety net was gone forever. I am not sure that I actually ever thought of her directly in this way while she was alive. Nevertheless, she had played this part in my life since birth, and now she was gone. I had to go on with the realization that this loving person who was always there for me, who always supported me, who was on my side and offered me a safe shoulder to cry on no matter what the circumstances, was no longer there.

While I have persevered and gone on with my life, adjusting to her absence, I am aware that an empty feeling is still with me. I miss her presence. Even though I still see her influence in the way I behave and in how I parent my children, there is a dimension of life that is gone, and I miss it. I miss her.

My mother was a kind person. Regardless of the circumstance, she could be counted on to be supportive and helpful to anyone in need. I remember how, after we three boys had grown up and moved away from home, she became involved in raising money for charities. She dedicated most of her energies to a Jewish charitable organization. People who raised some considerable sum for this charity were given a gold pin that represented the tablets of Moses. When we went through my mother's personal effects after her death, we were surprised to find three such pins. She had done this work without fanfare or self-aggrandizement. She had done it simply because it was the right thing to do and she lived by her principles.

For a number of years, my mother worked for a cookware company based in the Bronx near where we lived. She was not well educated, but she worked hard and rose to become the executive secretary for one of the owners. She enjoyed this job and did it well. In fact, she was so well liked that when the company was sold, the original owners made sure that she retained her job level and wages as part of the agreement. My mother adjusted to the change in ownership. Though she missed her former bosses, she set about doing the best job she could for the new executives. While I was never privy to the details, I learned that the new owners did not want to keep my mother in her job. Perhaps it was because she was not young or pretty, or maybe she could not keep up with the new demands. Whatever the reason, the new owners felt little loyalty to my mother. They treated her very badly, and eventually they fired her. My mother was upset about this, and she went through a period of self-doubt and mild depression. It did not last long, however, because she was resilient. Under such circumstances, most people would be hurt, angry, and bitter, and some would allow these feelings to affect them intensely over a long period. Not my mother. She rebounded quickly. Soon she was saying that, although she did not agree with the new owners' decision, she felt that they had done the best they could and had meant no malice.

This was the sort of person she was. She was so pleasant and optimistic that she could rise above adversity and not become bitter. This is an admirable trait that few people possess. I admire this about her, perhaps above all else. She was generous, forgiving, and good. I cannot remember her ever saying anything malicious, even out of justifiable anger, about any single individual. Rather, she labored to understand other people's reasoning and to give them the benefit of the doubt. It was this good-natured and positive attitude that characterized her life above all other qualities. She was not well educated, she was not a great beauty, she never made any great discoveries, but she had qualities that made her special. She was positive and optimistic and had faith in all people. How rare these qualities are! She was a person who could be counted on and relied on regardless of the circumstances. She would be nurturing, loving, and supportive.

Children learn a lot from their parents. Much of this is through modeling, watching what their parents do, rather than what they say, and emulating that behavior. While I do not profess to have gotten everything my mother displayed, I am aware that the better parts of me come largely from her.

Our life together was not exciting. In fact, it was quite mundane. The simple tasks of day-to-day living are what stick with me most. Going with her to shop at the neighborhood stores; sitting together watching television; going for walks: these are the memories I cling to when I think of my mother. The other night when I was channel surfing, flipping from one television station to another, I chanced upon a film that I had seen with my mother many years before. I can see in my mind's eye how we strolled arm in arm over to the bus stop. I can even remember the green plaid coat she wore. It made her look as if she had just come out of the north woods. On the bus, we sat side by side and chatted. The bus let us off directly in front of the theater. We both enjoyed the film. I remember noting the expression of avid interest in her profile as she leaned forward in the dark. Afterwards, we walked to an ice cream store and ordered the largest, gooiest hot fudge concoction on the menu with extra nuts on top and her favorite flavors, coffee and chocolate. Together, we eagerly devoured the mountain of ice cream. Then we took the same bus home and walked the two blocks to our apartment building, all the while chatting about the film. There was nothing exciting or unusual that makes this event stand out in my mind; I remember it because it is representative of being with my mother.

My mother had a creative side. Unfortunately, it was never expressed in a formalized manner. She never became an artist or writer. When she was younger, she considered studying fashion design, but her family was growing and she did not have the time to dedicate herself to a career. Instead, she found some rather unique ways of expressing herself. One way was in her style of dress. My mother did not go for conventional or designer clothing. Instead, she dressed creatively, with her own personal style and artistic flair. For example, when I was a child, most people would dress well for the theater. Men wore jackets and ties, and women wore formal dresses and jewelry. My mother was more daring – she would wear tall boots, black pants, a black top with enormous white polka dots, and a yellow scarf. This somehow worked for her. She not only looked appropriate, but quite elegant. Instead of a coat, she would don a cape. Pair this with her usual dramatic oversized glasses and big pieces of jewelry, and she was quite striking. Indeed, my mother always stood out. Just when you thought you understood her style, she would do something new that turned your conception upside down.

My mother also expressed her unique style in the way she decorated our apartment. When I was younger, I took the decor at home for granted. It always surprised me when friends from college who came to visit would comment on the eclectic nature of the objects my mother chose to display. Things would jump out at them that I no longer noticed. For example, she hung a Marc Chagall print near a traditional oil of a tranquil river scene. Across from these were some Japanese woodcuts. Mixed in were reproductions of old master drawings and some pictures of the family. To a purist, my mother's blend of things would be tantamount to heresy; to me, it was just home. Somehow, my mother had created a mixture that was, in a sense, artistic in itself, and it always got a reaction of some sort from visitors.

There are things you learn after someone has died that for some reason were never mentioned when they were alive. One thing I learned about my mother was that she had been an equestrian. When I was going through her things, I found her old riding boots in a closet under some bags, hidden away for who can say how long. I never saw my mother ride a horse. She never even mentioned that she knew how. My father could only recall that she used to ride before they were married, but he could not provide any details, and there is no one left to ask about this. As children, adult or otherwise, we have a rather skewed view of our parents. We somehow overlook the fact that they had a life before we entered it and went through the same developmental sequences we did. We forget that they also had a life away from us that we know little about. My mother rode horses, and I did not know that. Now I do, and I have several questions I would like to ask her that must remain unanswered.

Another thing I learned as I went through her possessions was that my mother had been a beauty contest winner – a queen of some pageant! I found a photograph that was unmistakably my mother, in a swimsuit, wearing a banner and a crown, holding flowers. Who thinks of their mother as a beauty queen? And she looked quite lovely! My father could only tell me what he had heard. Apparently, some friends had dared her to enter the contest. She was under the age limit, so she had to pretend to be 18. And she won! It was a great day for her — and, as it turned out, for the runner-up as well. The judges discovered that my mother was underage, and her crown was unceremoniously removed. Who would ever have thought that my dear, sweet, reliable mother could have had such an adventure? I regret not having the opportunity to know these parts of her life in more detail.

I got a glimpse of the secret side of my mother every once in a while, when it was her turn to have her friends over to play mah-jongg, a game that was quite popular in the Bronx in the fifties and sixties. The game rotated each week among her friends. Once every six weeks, it was held at our apartment. On that day, my mother would tidy things up and make sure the place was neat. We would eat dinner early, and then she would set up a bridge table and chairs and her large attaché-like mah-jongg case. She would set out refreshments — usually a cake and a pineapple and a big urn of coffee — and arrange everything beautifully for her friends. When they arrived, she would introduce us. We already knew them because we were friends with their children, but they never failed to comment on how big we were growing or how handsome we were. This was a little embarrassing, but it was part of the ritual. Then my mother and her friends would go into the den and shut the door and play for hours. We were usually asleep long before they stopped.

Strange words and noises came out of that room. As a young boy, I used to sneak up to and listen at the door, spying, trying to figure out just what they were doing. I would hear the strange clicking noise of the mah-jongg tiles being mixed around the table. Then they would begin to say strange things like "two crack" and "one bam." I can remember wondering if these phrases were some sort of secret code. They were, of course, simply the moves of the game. All the while, my mother and her friends would talk and tell stories, but I could not make out all of what they were saying. At times, gales of laughter would emanate from the room. They would literally get hysterical as they related various incidents and jokes. And I heard my mother's voice a lot! Apparently, she was quite the jokester and extremely lively. It was a side of her that I only saw on those Thursday nights when it was her turn to host mah-jongg. I can only wonder if perhaps she had other facets to her personality that I simply did not encounter.

What I did see was a gentle, nurturing person who always gave other people the benefit of the doubt. She always looked for the positive side of things, no matter what the circumstances. She somehow was able to pull herself out of anger and frustration and remain tolerant. When she died, a lot of people attended her funeral. Many were expected, family and close neighbors among them, but many were not. Several people came up to me to express their condolences, people whom I had never met, but who had loved and admired my mother. One woman came over and introduced herself, explaining that she had known my mother 30 years earlier. She had heard about her death and wanted to pay her respects. She had not seen my mother in all that time, but my mother had been so kind to her once during a stressful time that she wanted to attend her funeral. I don't know what it was that my mother had done for her, but whatever it was had remained in this woman's heart for 30 years. There were several other people who approached me on that day to express condolences and to reminisce about my mother. Each of them also had some story to tell about a kindness that my mother had done years earlier. These people did not forget her; she had lived in their memories for a long time.

My mother was a good person who tried to do the right thing for others whenever it was possible. Perhaps one indication of how successfully people have lived is how they are remembered when they die. People who make a lot of money are remembered for their wealth; people who are underhanded are remembered for the harm they have done. My mother, who was generous and kind, was remembered for her goodness, not only by family who loved her, but also by people who brushed against her even in the distant past. I was, indeed, very fortunate to have had such a person in my life. As odd as it sounds, I find it difficult to remember a single bad quality when I think of her. I suppose I could say that the way she did not take care of herself physically was a negative characteristic, for I would give just about anything to have had her handle this aspect of her life differently. As far as character is concerned, however, there was little to be faulted.

It has been some years since my mother died, yet there are moments when I go someplace that reminds me of her or hear a song she liked and I begin to think about her, and I miss her. I do see a lot of her influence in me. I see that I have passed some of this on to my own children, who are good people in their own right. My mother was and would be proud of them. Perhaps this is what is meant by continuity. Patterns of behaving are passed from generation to generation, and in that sense my mother still lives in me and in my children. Nevertheless, I would give just about anything to hear her voice, to feel her presence, or to get a hug from her one more time.

SUGGESTED READING

Aging in Society: Selected Reviews of Recent Research. L. Erlbaum Assoc., Hillsdale, NJ: 1983.

Aikin, Lewis R. Aging: An Introduction to Gerontology. Sage Publications, Thousand Oaks, CA: 1995.

Aikin, Lewis R. Later Life. L. Erlbaum Assoc., Hillsdale, NJ: 1989.

Atchley, Robert C. Aging, Continuity and Change. Wadsworth Publications, Belmont, CA: 1983.

Bliezner, Rosemary and Hillsevitch, Victoria, eds. Handbook on Aging and the Family. Greenwood Press, Westport, CT: 1995.

Booth, Wayne. The Art of Growing Older: Writers on Living and Aging. Poseidon Press, New York/London: 1992.

Bromley, D.B. Human Aging: An Introduction to Gerontology. Penguin Publications, London: 1988.

Brown, Arnold S. The Social Processes of Aging and Old Age. 2nd ed. Prentice Hall, Upper Saddle River, NJ: 1966.

Brown, Arnold S. The Social Processes of Aging and Old Age. Prentice Hall, Englewood Cliffs, NJ: 1990.

Chopra, Deepak. Ageless Body Timeless Mind. Random House Publishers, New York, NY: 1993.

Cicirelli, Victor G. Helping Elderly Parents: The Role of Adult Children. Auburn House, Boston, MA: 1981.

Cole, Thomas R. and Winkler, Mary G., eds. The Oxford Book of Aging. Oxford University Press, Oxford / New York: 1994.

Deren, Jane, ed. Portraits and Pathways: Exploring Stories of Aging. National Council on Aging, Washington, D.C.: 1988.

Edinberg, Mark A. Talking With Your Aging Parents. Shambhala, Boston, MA: 1987.

Fischer, David Hackett. Growing Old in America. Oxford University Press, Oxford / New York: 1978.

Geist, Harold. The Psychological Aspects of the Aging Process with Sociological Implications. 2nd ed. R.E. Krieger Publishing Co., Huntington, NY: 1981.

Greenberg, Vivian E. Your Best is Good Enough: Aging Parents and Your Emotions. Lexington Books, Lexington, MA: 1989.

Growing Old in America. 4th ed. Transaction Publishers, New Brunswick, NJ: 1991.

Halpern, James. Helping Your Aging Parents: A Practical Guide for Adult Children. McGraw-Hill, New York: 1987.

Handbook of the Biology of Aging. Academic Press, San Diego, CA: 1990.

Harris, Danna K. Sociology of Aging. Harper and Row, New York: 1990.

Hayflick, Leonard, Ph.D. How and Why We Age. Ballantine Books, New York: 1994.

Herbert, Anita S. Human Services for Older Adults: Concepts and Skills. University of South Carolina Press, Columbia, SC: 1990.

Hockey, Jennifer Lorna. Growing Up and Growing Old: Aging and Dependency in the Life Course. Sage Publications, London: 1993.

Hodkinson, H. M. Common Symptoms of Disease in The Elderly, 2nd ed. Oxford, England. Blackwell Scientific Publications, St. Louis, MO: 1980.

How to Care for Your Parents, A Handbook for Adult Children. Storm King Press, Washington, D.C.: 1987.

Jacobsen, Jamia Jasper. Help! I'm Parenting My Parents. Benchmark Press, Indianapolis, IN: 1988.

Jarvik, Lissy, M.D., Ph.D., and Small, Gary, M.D. Parentcare: A Commonsense Guide for Adult Children. Crown Publishers, New York: 1988.

Koch, Tom. <u>Aging Children and Elderly Parents</u>. Praeger Press, New York: 1990.

Kübler-Ross, Elizabeth. <u>On Death and Dying</u>. MacMillan Publishing, New York: 1969.

Levin, Nora Jean. <u>How to Care for Your Parents: A Handbook for Adult Children</u>. Storm King Press, Washington, D.C.: 1987.

Mall, E. Jane. <u>How to Care for Your Elderly Mother and Stay Sane</u>. Ballantine Books, New York, NY: 1990.

McKee, Patrick and Thiem, Jon, eds. <u>Real Life: Ten Stories of Aging</u>. University Press of Colorado, Miwot, CO: 1994.

Myers, Edward. <u>When Parents Die: A Guide for Adults</u>. Penguin Press, New York, NY: 1987.

Pables, Ronald; Gift, Helen C.; and Ory, Marcia G., eds. <u>Aging and the Quality of Life</u>. Springer Series on Lifestyles and Issues in Aging, Springer Publishing, New York: 1994.

Posner, Richard A. <u>Aging and Old Age</u>. University of Chicago Press, Chicago, IL: 1995.

Schaie, K. Warner and Schooler, Corni, eds. <u>Social Structure and Aging: Psychological Processes</u>. L. Erlbaum Assoc., Hillsdale, NJ: 1989.

Shephard, Roy J. <u>Physical Activity and Aging</u>. Aspen Publishers, Rockville, MD: 1987.

Watson, Wilbur H. <u>Aging and Social Behavior: An Introduction to Social Gerontology</u>. Wadsworth Health Sciences Division, Monterey, CA: 1982.

Woodruff-Pak, Dana. <u>Psychology and Aging</u>. Prentice-Hall, Inc., New Jersey: 1988.

Zins, Sandra. <u>Aging in America: An Introduction to Gerontology</u>. Delmar Publishers, Albany, NY: 1987.